Assorted Stories
*Through the Eyes of a Small Town Lawyer*

# Criminals Cheats & Liars

Judge James P. Sheehy

Updated: January, 2014

# Table of Contents

| | | |
|---|---|---|
| Introduction | | v |
| Chapter One | The *Corpus Delicti* Rule | 1 |
| Chapter Two | Going in Cold | 15 |
| Chapter Three | Luck of the Draw | 29 |
| Chapter Four | B&E Boys | 44 |
| Chapter Five | Malevolent Prosecutions | 53 |
| Chapter Six | Avoid Trouble | 73 |
| Chapter Seven | Youngsters | 85 |
| Chapter Eight | Neutral Judges | 95 |
| Chapter Nine | The Gambler | 107 |
| Chapter Ten | Youthful Dream | 119 |
| Chapter Eleven | Offensive Judges | 129 |
| Chapter Twelve | Professor Keenan | 139 |
| Chapter Thirteen | Doctor Death | 149 |
| Chapter Fourteen | Everyone's Lincoln | 167 |
| Chapter Fifteen | A Good Friend | 181 |
| Chapter Seventeen | Good Cop/Bad Cop | 199 |
| Chapter Eighteen | The Boxer | 217 |
| Chapte Nineteen | Sentencing | 233 |
| Chapter Twenty | The Jury and the Pub | 245 |
| Chapter Twenty-One | Try Mediation | 255 |
| Chapter Twenty-Two | Walk Straight | 267 |
| Conclusion | | 277 |
| Acknowledgments | | 287 |

# Introduction

*You told me this,*
*You told me that*
*You try to tell me,*
*Tell me where it's at*
*You said you loved me,*
*I can see through that...*
*Lies, lies, lies*
                     J. J. Cale

---

I first wrote this compilation of stories to serve as a primer for students who may be interested in taking up Law as a career, only to find that students are too busy to read a book of like this. I started out the Introduction this way:

"If you have ever considered a career in the world of law, this book is for you. Many students aspire to attend law school and/or develop a career in the field of law. Sharing my private practice in the law and many years on the bench may be invaluable to you in making a well thought out career choice and having a successful career."

A professor of English and Editor of a major university press reviewed this book and confirmed that it probably was not for students; but she sure enjoyed the read.

In the great portrait of Life, these Assorted Stories represent but a few brush strokes of my life's work. So here we go...

The world I grew up in was much different from my parents' world. In fact, today's world is much different than it was just a few years ago. My grandfather fought in the Civil War. My father played professional baseball for the St. Louis Browns. My mother was a passenger on the first airplane flight at the Cleveland Air Show. Computers were a novelty in my college years and Dick Tracy was a cartoon strip. Ideas that I could only imagine back then, today are called applications and easily accessible on my iPhone. As life moves ever faster, changes in lifestyle such as these will grow exponentially during your lifetime.

It all began in a quiet northwest neighborhood of Detroit, Michigan. Events I experienced in those days and later in my career, I share with you at the beginning of each chapter. Many of the stories are humorous; but all are unique. *These personal Sidebar stories are <u>separate and distinct</u> from those that follow in each chapter. In Journalism, a Sidebar is a brief story on a sidelight to a news story, such as a biographical sketch about a figure in the news or an anecdote related to the main story. In the Law, Sidebar is an area in front of or next to the judge's bench where lawyers are called to speak confidentially with the judge out of earshot of the jury.*

All the events in this quasi-memoir are based on my lifetime experiences. However, the settings every so often are fictionalized or composited and many names are changed to protect the innocent, as they say.

After sixteen years of formal education and three years in law school, I accepted a clerkship with the Chief Justice of the Michigan Supreme Court. My next stop was the City of Rochester, Michigan, where I established a general practice of law. I provided my regular clients representation in real estate transactions, divorces, estate planning and criminal defense. Some of my many corporate clients included the K-Mart Corporation, the Township of Pontiac (City of Auburn Hills) and its Economic Development Corporation. In 1981, I became Judge of the Michigan District Court. I served for nineteen years a community of about 180,000 residents living in one-quarter of Oakland County (approx. 200 sq. miles). After leaving the bench in 2000, I became an arbitrator, certified mediator and senior visiting judge for the next ten years.

The world in which I chose to practice law covered the full spectrum of society. My wonderful neighbors provided a decent and proper clientele. Those in need allowed me to act as their public defender. During all those years, I tried to sidestep the criminals, cheats and liars lurking out there in their unregulated wasteland.

JPS

# Chapter One

# The *Corpus Delicti* Rule

*A seminal point in my life was the death of my father. That was in the third grade. Later in the same year, my family moved to another part of the city necessitating a new school, new friends and the beginning of a new life. I found myself often visiting with the fathers of my friends.*

*The father of a grade-school friend Joe worked hard to provide for his family. He would go off to work every morning and come home at the same time each afternoon like most other dads. I did not know then, as a kid, that Joe's father was a "bookie," a highly regarded bookmaker who never bound a book, but could give you the odds on every sporting event in town. He had an office in a pool hall in the southeast side of town. All the dads had jobs, whether it was off to the steel mill, the car assembly plant or in the hospitality business. Most bookmakers in the United States merely bet on college and professional sports, but Joe's dad specialized in the daily horse races and also took in numbers slips on the side. The inner city folks can go down to the drug store and buy a "Dream Book" to help them in selecting their lucky numbers, but they need someone reliable who will take their action and give them decent odds. Those blue-collar working folks are only seeking their piece of the American Dream.*

*To be continued...*

---

After sixteen years of formal education and three years in law school, I accepted a clerkship with the Chief Justice of the Michigan Supreme Court. I lived in the capital city for a year reviewing and rewriting judicial opinions. During that time, the Supreme Court staff attorneys performed *pro bono* legal work across the street in the Ingham County Circuit Court. I took over a murder case right out of the chute and received the time necessary to handle it. It dawned on me, however, that I needed to be first sworn in as an attorney, before I could officially practice law.

The Admission to the Bar Ceremony is a very special moment for the candidate, as well as his family. The Honorable James L. Ryan, Judge of the Circuit Court, serving Wayne County, Michigan, agreed to perform the swearing-in formality. A friend of our family Edward J. Parker was kind enough to move my admission to the bar before the court. Ed and his lovely wife Eleanor were classmates of my mother many years earlier at Flora Stone Mather College in Cleveland. Mr. Parker said to Judge Ryan, "I might say how long I have known this boy, I guess I knew him the day he was born and as such, we have to give him a lot of credit because he did this with the help of his mother and she is here today."

Judge Ryan followed, "Thank you, Mr. Parker. I certainly agree that no young man can ever appreciate the accomplishment of membership in the Bar Association. By that I mean, he cannot really appreciate and enjoy the privilege it is to complete his legal education until he has a real understanding of the role his parents have played in that program; and some of us, and I use the word 'us' advisedly, Mr. Sheehy—can thank our mother more dearly, more immediately than others of us. Therefore, today is an important day. I am aware of your work with the Chief Justice Brennan in the Supreme Court and the role you played shortly after your completion of your formal studies. You have been recommended highly for admission to the Bar and in that recommendation, of course, this court personally concurs. I want to congratulate you on the completion of your studies and I extend my congratulations to your family."

With that, Judge Ryan administered the oath of office, swearing me in as an attorney to practice law throughout all of the courts in the state, concurrent with the privilege to practice in the United States District Court.

*****

The law of the land in most states has for its foundation the Common Law of England, with the exception of the State of Louisiana where the basis of their legal system comes by way of France and the Napoleonic Code. The common law is the unwritten law; it was developed over the years by word of mouth until legislatures codified the laws with written statutes. Common Law is the traditional law of England.

The man accused of murder was David Wayne Tweed. "Your Honor, my name is James P. Sheehy and I am here to represent Mr. Tweed. This matter comes before this honorable court for the purpose of conducting a preliminary examination."

"Thank you Mr. Sheehy," the judge responded. "Let me explain what this hearing is about, so that we are all on the same page. A preliminary examination is a probable cause hearing. The court must make a determination whether, based on competent evidence presented and received by this court, the elements of a crime are present and if sufficient probable cause exists for one to believe the defendant committed the crime. The standard I will use in my determination is based on the preponderance of evidence," the judge said.

Here are the facts in the case before the court. Donald Vance died 20 years ago and his body became a county medical examiner's case. After an autopsy and a review of the resulting evidence, two medical examiners determined the manner of his death was from "natural causes" and not any form of homicide. Vance's cremation closed the book on his life's story, or so everyone thought.

Some 20 years later, the City Police received a letter from David Wayne Tweed regarding Vance's death, in which he wrote clearly that he killed Vance years ago. The letter originated from the state prison where Mr. Tweed was serving a life sentence for a previous murder conviction. In a follow-up interview, the police obtained a confession in which Tweed repeated that he killed Donald Vance.

For an extra-judicial confession to be admissible, the prosecution must first establish, without the use of that confession, the deceased Donald Vance was murdered and his death was not a result of natural causes as the original medical examiners indicated in their autopsy report. In short, the prosecutor had an uphill battle to prove their own medical examiners were wrong the first time they reported on Donald Vance's death. This rule of law is The *Corpus Delicti* Rule.

The police sent Tweed's confession to a new medical examiner who made new findings. In his response letter he said this. "Pursuant to [the meeting with the police] and Tweed's written communication...[he] reviewed the [20 year old] autopsy report issued by Drs. Davenport and Brooks, the autopsy photographs, the death scene photographs" and amended the manner of death on the official Death Certificate to "Homicide." He added the immediate cause of death as Asphyxia; how the injury occurred, "smothered by other." Not so coincidently, just as Weed's confession stated.

Curiously, this new medical examiner was never able to conduct an autopsy on the deceased or consider past medical history, since Mr. Vance's body had been cremated at the time of his death. As a result, the medical doctor was unable to draw any medical conclusions about the cause of death by means of laboratory examination of body fluids, cell samples or tissues. He did not prepare a report of his own, known as a protocol or an autopsy report.

I researched the issues in the case and found a recent law review article named In Defense of the Corpus Delicti Rule, written by Assistant Professor David A. Moran of Wayne State University Law School, Detroit, Michigan; 64 Ohio State Journal 817, in which he set out the law. He wrote:

> "The common law *corpus delicti* rule prohibits the introduction of an extra judicial confession in a judicial case unless the prosecution introduces independent evidence of the 'corpus delicti.' (body of the crime) That is, the prosecution must introduce some evidence independent of the confession that the crime described actually occurred."

> "This article reviews a Michigan Appeals case named *People v. McAllister* to "show how the corpus delicti rule can prevent miscarriages of justice in cases to which other confession doctrines do not apply at all." In that case, McAllister's baby, Daniel, died in his sleep. A pathologist and a local medical examiner performed an autopsy, and each concluded that Daniel had died of Sudden Infant Death Syndrome (SIDS). Both physicians agreed that they found no evidence of criminality or any kind of trauma to Daniel..."

McAllister, whose mental illness deteriorated following the loss of her son, later told her psychiatrist that she killed her son in a satanic sacrifice. The Michigan State Police charged her with the murder of her son, after extracting a confession from her.

> "The pathologist and the medical examiner who had performed the autopsy, not only testified during the trial that Daniel, in their opinion, died of SIDS, but also that all physical signs of internal suffocation that one would expect to find were completely absent from the autopsy."

The appellate court observed, *"McAllister* is a straightforward *corpus delicti* case."

The facts in the David Tweed murder case paralleled the *McAllister* case until the current medical examiner stuck his nose into the case and changed the death certificate. The role of a medical examiner differs from that of the non-physician coroner in that the medical examiner is expected to bring medical expertise to the evaluation of the medical history and physical examination of the deceased. Clearly, this new medical examiner knew nothing about the dead man.

It was time for a little logic. The medical examiner's testimony set up a syllogism wherein **A+B=C**. The Michigan Rules of Evidence, Rule 702 and Rule 703, without a doubt, controlled the testimony of the medical examiner. **A**: "In consideration of the photographic evidence from the scene of death and the postmortem exam...the cause of death is asphyxia." **B**: The body turned and "smothered by another." **C**: "The manner of death is amended to homicide." However, it did not. The answer to the legalistic rhyme was in my handbook on evidence and exposes this flawed theory.

"Courtroom Handbook on Michigan Evidence: 703.1: The Rational of the Rule"

"Rule 703 sets forth the criteria that govern the factual basis of the testimony of the expert witness. The amendment of the Rule represented a sea change in the procedure for admitting expert testimony in Michigan courts. Unless the underlying facts are actually admitted in evidence, an expert may no longer offer opinion based on facts supplied to him or her by others, even if such facts are of the kind normally relied upon by the expert in his or her everyday practice...

"The rational for adopting this strict procedure was to eliminate the practice of introducing inadmissible hearsay through the device of having an expert explain the basis for his or her opinion."

The medical examiner said, "The deceased's body was turned and smothered by another." That conclusion is not supported with any facts placed into evidence. The medical examiner's opinion was purely illusionary. Since proof of "**B**" is mere suspicion, but for the admissions of Mr. Tweed, "**C**" the manner of death is "Homicide" becomes a nullity. This examiner was all wet and his testimony did not make any legal sense because he had no admissible evidence to support this conclusion. I started feeling good just about this time in the case and my confidence grew by the minute and by the witness.

The medical examiner testified he changed the cause of death to asphyxia. The Merriam Webster Medical Dictionary defines Asphyxia as, "a lack of oxygen or excess of carbon dioxide in the body that results in unconsciousness and often death and is usually caused by interruption of breathing or inadequate breathing supply." Once again, the medical examiner's conclusion that the cause of the asphyxia here was by smothering was merely a guess and most probably based on Weed's statement to the police.

In addition to all of these hypothetical conclusions, the medical examiner went off on a tangent to interject his personal criticism of the only autopsy report by claiming the doctors trivialized the importance of the trauma sustained by the deceased. By simply viewing pictures, he described the deceased as having blunt force trauma to the forehead. The first medical examiners, however, conducted an autopsy of the body within 24 hours of the death. They removed parts of the body, weighed and tested them and reduced their medical findings to an autopsy report in which they stated, "Evidence of injury is manifested by a 1½" superficial abrasion the left forehead and a ½" superficial linear abrasion the hairline on the left scalp."

You can be sure, if the original medical examiners had found a blunt force trauma, they would have reported it. They did not. They reported superficial abrasions, contrary to the current examiner's conclusion. The original medical examiners had the benefit of the body; the current doctor did not. The current examiner continued his criticism of the original examiners' approach as an "off the cuff diagnosis" attempting to discredit their work product in order to support his unfounded position. That is not the role of the medical examiner.

From the case reported by Professor Moran, I was also aware of certain medical procedures in an autopsy used to determine asphyxia. The original medical examiners' autopsy and protocol was complete on its face and supported their conclusions. All physical signs of internal suffocation that one would expect to find were completely absent from the autopsy. The current doctor's medical conclusions turned out to be more hypothetical make believe and not supported by any post mortem examination of the deceased.

Common sense and deductive logic took over as I began my argument to the Court that there was just no evidence of a crime presented by the assistant prosecutor handling the case. I closed my comments by saying, "From the beginning, we see that the original manner of death was properly determined to be 'Natural'. Moreover, for 20 years this classification was satisfactory and left untouched, until the defendant contacted the City Police Department. Together with the admissions and a purported confession, the police presented this information to current medical examiner. At this point, the doctor armed himself with the information he needed to change the death record. He was unable to determine that the deceased died from asphyxia just by looking at pictures; he could only guess at it, since the pictures portrayed the deceased face down on a pillow. How could the doctor take the next step and say the asphyxia was 'smothered by another' and not by choking or strangulation or carbon dioxide inhalation or seizure or sleep apnea or drug overdose, unless he first had access and knowledge of the statements the defendant gave to the police? How could he conclude the death was homicide without any new medical evidence? It is impossibility."

The assistant prosecutor was dumbfounded by my argument. His position was the defendant confessed to the crime. What else did he need to prove his case? The Court wasted no time and simply ruled, "The corpus delicti rule renders the statements of the Defendant Tweed inadmissible and they are hereby suppressed. Without the statements, there is no case. This matter is closed for lack of admissible evidence."

I sat back and took a deep breath. I had won my first lawsuit on an age-old common law theory. I later found out Mr. Tweed was goofier than a cat on drugs, just plain legally crazy. The *corpus delicti* rule was created to prevent just this type of person from being convicted based on his or her own statements alone.

Caution: Please remember that each state interprets or defines this rule differently. The Federal Courts no longer use the *corpus delicti* rule because they believe defendants have a sufficient number of rights like the

*Miranda Rule* with which they can use to defend themselves.

This case may not receive the same judicial decision in another court or from another judge. Not all judges are created equal, yet the law should be applied equally to all of us. You will see in the next chapter that you need to know and understand every judge you come before in court.

**And then there is this...**
I said in the Introduction, "All the events in this quasi-memoir are based on my lifetime experiences. However, the settings every so often are fictionalized or composited and many names are changed to protect the innocent, as they say."

Chapter One, The *Corpus Delicti* Rule is a powerful story of one of the basic laws first in England and later in the United States. Simply stated; a crime cannot be based solely on an admission statement of an individual.

Because of its importance, I placed this story first in the book along with my being sworn-in as a lawyer. I portrayed the story from the view of a defense attorney. That part was a fictionalization to make the story fit in.

In reality, here is what happened. During the year 2008, I was asked to serve parts of twenty-three weeks as a senior visiting judge in the City of Pontiac. One day as I concluded the assigned traffic cases and criminal arraignments at 10 a.m. in the morning, the assignment clerk entered the courtroom with the file of *People v. Donald Vance*, a preliminary hearing on First Degree Murder.

I advised all the parties to the case I would render my Opinion in thirty days, after hearing the testimony in the case during the remainder of the day. Chapter One is that Opinion, word for word.

Two matters the reader may find interesting.

As a visiting judge, I was not provided with the assistance of a research clerk or an updated set of law books with which to aid in the preparation of my Opinion. One day during the lunch hour, I headed over the county law library. It had been nine years since I retired and very few librarians knew me. I asked for the **2008** version of the Courtroom Handbook on Michigan Evidence and found that during the year of 2003, the Michigan Supreme Court made a significant change in Rule 702, which was described in Rule 703.1 as a "sea change in the procedure of admitting expert testimony in Michigan."

The disposition of the case revolved around the change in this Rule of Evidence. Interestingly enough, I discussed the ruling with the other judges in the courthouse after my decision was published and none were aware of the rule change. By the end of the year, I no longer felt I was as current and up-to-date on the changes in the state of the law since retiring and chose to no longer sit as a visiting judge. My days on the bench came to an end.

Another interesting fact I learned was that any county medical examiner in Michigan has full discretion to change a death certificate for any reason and there is no review of such a change. As you read in Chapter One, the medical examiner changed the cause of death based upon the admission of Donald Vance and a review of the pictures of the death scene. This is the same medical examiner that overlooked or missed hypodermic needle marks on Dr. Kevorkian's victims 2 & 3. This will give more meaning to Chapter Thirteen, Dr. Death.

## Chapter Two

## Going in Cold

*The bookmaker's role, apart from attracting his customers, is the adjustment of the odds in his favor or having a point spread that ensures a balanced book. They say that a balanced book insures a favorable profit margin for the bookie at the end of the day.*

*Joe's well-appreciated father had the reputation of paying off his winners within twenty-four hours of posting the winning numbers. Historically, there have been famous bookies. In the forties for example, Boston's Fanna Ryan and his son Tommy, every year at Christmastime, would hand out gift certificates for large turkeys to over 250 of their best customers. All the bettors had to do to cash in these chits was to stop by the finest and friendly Premium Market on Massachusetts Avenue in downtown Cambridge to pick up the birds, a grocery store where Fanna had made those arrangements. This was a win-win for everybody.*

*Those days are gone. Now the government is the "big brother" bookmaker. You can go over to any gas station and pick your own numbers on two or three daily games or you can have the computer randomly select your numbers. The state was not operating Power Ball or Mega Bucks games back then. Joe's dad had an honest edge on his competition because the winning numbers always came from the numbers of the second horse to finish in the first five races of the day.*

*In the early years of Detroit's history, the major influence on the legal community came from the Irish residents. Most of the cops were Irish, sometimes spanning three or four generations. Many of the judges in Detroit also carried an Irish moniker. Stories were abundant about those "Mc" judges and how they dealt out their cards of justice. I remember a judge named "West Side Red." Every year in the spring, Judge Reddy would put on a black-tie dinner dance for the benefit of the Loving Sisters of St Jean. Because of Reddy's prominent position as Chief Judge, every lawyer and politician in the tri-county area felt obligated to show up with their spouses and enjoy the dinner and live music. Michigan law forbids sitting judges from raising money for their re-election campaigns in other than election years. There are no limits on donations for charitable fundraisers though. Since this was a benefit for the good sisters, nobody gave a second thought to Judge Reddy's intentions. Every year the dinner dance grew larger and more successful, raising thousands and thousands of dollars, until Reddy retired from the bench.*

*Then the word started to dribble out that there was no such order of Catholic nuns named the Loving Sisters. "On behalf of the good Sisters, Judge Reddy Thanks You" read his thank you notes faithfully sent out within a week of each event on courthouse stationary. Judge Reddy was manipulating with the system for the benefit of his good old campaign fund. While everyone thought Judge Reddy was thanking all for the Sisters, he was really thanking all for benefiting him.          To be continued...*

---

Growing up, I worked at just about every job anyone my age could have, short of being a dockworker on the Great Lakes. In most of the jobs, my boss would tell me what to do and leave me to complete the work as directed. I had a reputation of "just show me once and I will get it done." Of all the various jobs worked in high school and college, I worked in two different grocery stores. One was an old A&P food store near the college campus. The job entailed restocking the grocery shelves from 11:30 pm and 7:30 am. I was the only student I knew with this kind of schedule.

During my law school years, I worked for an insurance company as a claim adjuster. My supervisor at Traveler's Insurance claim department was Ed Mattingly, a lawyer who understood my being a law student; that is, working full time and taking a full complement of classes. I relied on Ed teaching me the ins and outs of the insurance claims business. Ed was a licensed attorney, but practiced his profession only in the Traveler's office. I met other law students also working their way through law school, as I moved around through various departments in the office, i.e. life insurance and worker's compensation and general liability. For a three-year period, I established a new set of friends and had an opportunity to socialize with them some weeknights. It was sad to leave these friends when I moved to the capital city to work for the Supreme Court, but that is part of life; moving on and moving up.

An older lawyer who lived across the street offered me some sound advice once. "Stick with the job you have and do not move around from one job to another." Stability in the work force was an important element in my neighbor's opinion. Today's young workers, it is predicted, will have three or four careers in their working life, let alone three of four different jobs.

At the Supreme Court, I was given an office cubicle, somewhat isolating me from the others. All the workers in this department had at least two degrees, one being a law degree. Everyone generally understood his or her role and the timing constraints regarding the court's written opinions. People were pleasant with each other, but there was none of the socializing which I became accustomed to at the insurance company.

One of my jobs was to travel with the Chief Justice and make sure the judge had all the materials he needed for his next meeting or speech. The "CJ" often complimented me by calling me the best lackey (helper) he ever had. I never took that comment the wrong way. I always smiled and said, "thank you sir." The secretaries throughout the building held everything together like an anchor connected solidly to a ship. They all knew each other, even though they worked specifically for separate justices. They interacted well together to make the Supreme Court run smoothly. They kept their confidence within the office, while being kind and helpful to everyone else. The clerk's office was always jumping with activity because they are the office open to the public. They could find any form or a case file rapidly and they appeared to the outside to truly enjoy their work.

The six associate justices kept to themselves and all were distinguished men and women in their own right. I became a close friend, much like a son, to Justice Thomas Giles Kavanagh. There was a second Justice named Thomas M. Kavanagh on the same bench at the time. He was from the small town of Carson City and served from 1958 to 1975. Thomas Matthew Kavanagh the hard driving, politically astute, long-time Chief Justice was aptly called in political spheres "Thomas the Mighty" and Thomas Giles Kavanagh was known as "Thomas the Good". Close friends and colleagues always referred to Thomas Giles as just plain "Giles".

*****

When I started my private practice of law, it was a new ballgame with more people and more names to learn. I needed to create my own scorecard. While the practice of law takes one out to many counties and jurisdictions, the majority of an individual's practice is mainly located in the county where his office is located. I found myself practicing law at the Oakland County courthouse at least three days a week. One of my first new friends became Judge William Beasley, a kind and caring judge. Judges understand that new attorneys need a little direction and Judge Beasley was one of the best in lending a guiding hand. There were all sorts of people in the courthouse who were also helpful, from the clerk's office, the court administrator's office to each judges' personal staff. John Mayer was the court administrator in the circuit court when I started practicing.

The State of Michigan had recently changed the marriage laws from "fault" divorce to "no-fault" divorce. One needed only to confirm in court that a breakdown of the marriage occurred in order to receive a judgment of divorce.

There was an old-time judge by the name of Arthur Moore, who would give you the impression he had been on the bench since the invention of the internal combustion engine. He just could not grasp this change in the divorce laws and consequently would not grant any divorce judgments without pleading and proving the former statutory faults. I appeared one day before Judge Moore to obtain an uncontested *pro-confesso* divorce. Judge Moore would not grant the divorce without a showing of adultery or some other legislative fault in the marriage. I shook my head, walked out into the hallway where I bumped into John Mayer, the above mentioned court administrator. John and I became friends earlier so I explained to him my plight. John took my client and me down the hall into another courtroom that was in session. He approached the judge during a break and whispered something to him. My case was called next and a decree of final divorce was granted, just as smooth and quickly as could be. This was a clear sign of a good relationship.

When a new client walks into a law office with legal papers in his hand, the first question any good attorney will ask is to which judge is your case assigned? Knowing the answer allows a lawyer to plan his approach to the case from that point going forward. The Honorable Francis X. O'Brien was the most affable person you could meet in a public setting. However, when he put on his judge's robe and assumed the bench, he turned into an argumentative judge, inserting himself and his personal feelings into almost every case. Judge Frank O'Brien often times spun out of control in court. His older brother, John was also a circuit judge, occupying a courtroom just down the hall from Frank. John was my mentor for a number of years. He liked to work his way home to Royal Oak by stopping at many local neighborhood pubs and campaigning, if you will, by having a few drinks with the local voters. It was often said of the brother judges, "The more John drank; the crazier Frank became in his rulings from the bench."

For another example, I found out two judges were treating for some psychiatric disorders—a well-known fact throughout the courthouse. These particular judges always had smiles on their faces, but down deep, they were time bombs ready to explode at the slightest movement of the Richter scale. With these two judges, no one ever knew which side of the bed they got up from each morning or how they would react to any slightest comment. All attorneys recognized them as hallowed beings in their courtrooms and treaded softly on eggshells so as not to provoke any reason to set them off.

One day I was before one of them with an important case representing a senior citizen charged with exposing himself to his granddaughter. That act never happened, but the nature of the case was so sensitive and fragile anything could knock it off the centerline. At one point, I was following a particular procedural rule when the judge corrected me with his version of the same rule. Not really thinking this through at that moment, I quickly rebutted the judge setting off his patented red-face stare-down. The judge then opened his bench rulebook to, in a sense, rub my nose in it. He found my version of the rule to be the correct one. The judge continued his stern stare and slowly said, "OK, Mr. Sheehy, you may continue." That is about as close as I ever came to losing a case for my client and sending him off to jail. My politeness went a long way. The client returned to his retirement home in Florida and his case was ultimately dismissed without a trial.

Judges are unique unto themselves and do not forget it. One of the most inimitable judges was William John Beer. When I first saw his name on the courtroom door, I thought of my fellow classmate named Tom Beer. This Judge Beer was from a different Beer family residing out of Berkley, Michigan. I had no warning about Judge Beer's mannerisms before the first time I sat in his courtroom. He gave the impression of a kind and compassionate man who was concerned for everyone's welfare, by all outward appearances. Judge Beer was the only judge in the state who imposed an age old legal prohibition from remarrying for one year after granting a divorce. He lectured those seeking a divorce more severely than one might receive from a member of the clergy. Once he started, the homily seemed never to end. He always concluded his divorce speech by saying, "You may be divorcing each other, but you can never divorce your children." When the discourse ended, Judge Beer penalized the now divorced couple with a one-year lawful restriction on remarrying.

Mrs. Byrd was Judge Beer's secretary for many years. I would stick my head into her office and say hello, as I passed through the courthouse. Once I filed a lawsuit against the department of motor vehicles in the Secretary of State's office for the return my client's driver's license. His driving privilege was suspended for a period because of an auto accident. Judge Beer was the judge assigned to the case. While each circuit judge then had the authority to reinstate drivers' licenses, Beer always refused to do so for some unknown reason. Everyone knew this was one of the judge's quirks. I advised my client to forget about getting his license back and placed his file back into my desk drawer. I did not want to waste any more of my client's money. About three months later, Mrs. Byrd called telling me the judge would be out of town next week and I should schedule driver's license restoration case while the he was gone. At court the next week, a visiting judge in Judge Beer's absence reinstated my client's driving privileges. That my friend is how it works!

I would be remiss in not telling you another well-known fact about Judge Beer. He enjoyed leaving court early and driving into the City of Detroit to attend the Detroit Tigers baseball games. He also loved to sit as a visiting judge in the City of Detroit, as often as he could. Many of the county employees who worked daily in the Oakland County courthouse including Mrs.

Byrd and Marguerite, the judge's court reporter, had full knowledge that Judge Beer had something else going on in Detroit. It was not until after the judge retired, however, that the newspapers revealed Judge Beer was living a double life. He had a second wife and raised a second family of five children in a home near Indian Village in the City of Detroit; while at the same time, being married to his first wife and using her Oakland County address to maintain his judicial position. This bizarre story of bigotry later became the subject for a made-for-television motion picture. Clearly, Judge Beer's personal and professional life was an example of high hypocrisy, with no redeeming value whatsoever. He became a disservice to the legal profession and he made a mockery of the judiciary.

So now you can see, when called upon to represent a client in any particular court, knowing which judge has been assigned to a case and then knowing the background of that judge enhances your chances of success. Going in cold just won't do it.

**And then there is this...**
In Chapter Thirteen, I refer to the then elected county prosecutor Dick Thompson as Dickie Tompkins saying, "He went to law school and later became the prosecutor in the county. He was a conservative sort of prosecutor; some would say a little to the right of Glenn Beck. He had no trouble prosecuting anything that moved. In fact, it seemed to him the court system was

nothing but a hindrance to his effort to eradicate crime from the streets of the county. Try to fix in your mind an image of a gallows constructed behind Tomkins's office and you may get the picture."

In Chapter Two, I believed that you needed to know as much as you could about the judge you may be going before on a case or any type of motion practice. A good example is when I represented Dorothy Sites (Chapter Five) who was summarily fired by Orion Township for theft. It was my experience that an employee should usually have a hearing before being dismissed from their employment position. Dorothy was denied that hearing. My first step was to obtain such a hearing. I filed my first and only civil lawsuit in the Federal District Court. Proud of myself, I looked forward to being in the Federal Courthouse downtown pleading my case for justice. Within a week, I received a written Order from the Honorable Cornelia Kennedy granting my request for a due process hearing. It was up to the Township to decide the forum for the hearing. The Township simply placed Dorothy Sites on the agenda of the next public meeting, disregarding all of the confidentiality that goes along with personnel matters. (See page 54)

As I traveled from court to court, I began to notice a pattern of how particular judges made their various rulings. I concluded, if the decision was controversial or political, the judge would most often bail out and rule in favor of the People (the prosecution). As a practicing attorney in all of the county courts, I found that the many judges seemed to be intimidated by the county prosecutor's office. Clear and unarguable motions for the defense would be debated and a judge often would waive the defense attorney off gratuitously while denying the relief requested. A local judge once told me that he was tired of the conflict with the prosecutor and decided to give them (the prosecutor's office) anything they wanted. He said they were in his court every day and he could no longer take their pressure.

From the days I took the bench, I began to notice the subliminal pressure presented to the court by the office of the prosecutor. If a court failed to rule for the prosecution in certain cases, a notice of appeal would be filed and sent to the sitting judge. One night an investigator from the Prosecutor's Office drove to my home to serve me Motion papers, just for the purpose of intimidation. I did not answer the door and phoned the Sherriff's department. Within five minutes, the street in front of my home was filled with police cars. The investigator was ushered off my property and out of the subdivision.

I enjoyed walking through the main clerk's office in the morning to welcome our employees and wish them a great day. Early on in my first term, I noticed a five-drawer file cabinet off to the side that seemed unused.

I found, upon further inspection, the drawers were full of thin manila folders. I asked what this was about and was told these folders contained unexecuted misdemeanor complaints prepared from time to time by assistant prosecutors and city attorneys. They counted in the hundreds; piling up over the years and there were no plans to do anything with them. Just let them sit there and rot.

I suggested we return them to their creators or maybe close out the files with a notation "No further action taken." My mode of efficiency stirred up a nest of hornets. The county prosecutor's office, under the direction of Dickie Tomkins, quickly filed a lawsuit against me personally, and not the Court, prompting headlines in the next day's paper that read: *Judge Dismisses Hundreds of Criminal Cases*. This was the start of prosecutorial pressure on the new judge.

Remember when I cautioned that you cannot go into any court cold. You must know your players. This bullying lawsuit was assigned to the Honorable James S. Thorburn (see Chapter Twenty-One). I knew Judge Thorburn very well, having practiced before him for eleven years. I knew his likes and dislikes and who his friends were. I hired attorney Joe Hardig, the Birmingham lawyer and close friend of Judge Thorburn to defend me in this case. I was confident this litigation was going nowhere. Later Joe Hardig suggested to me that I set all of those inactive folders for a public hearing and notify the press. The prosecutors and city attorneys were invited to comment and present on the record any reasons to continue hanging on to these old dog cases.

All the folder cases were closed once again, after a full and fair hearing in open court. The first salvo of court intimidation missed its mark, but there would be more to follow as the years went on.

# Chapter Three
# Luck of the Draw

*The practice of law is more than a business, it is a profession. When one is in trouble, a lawyer may be the best person to assist you with a predicament and set you on a straight and narrow again. Frequently you do not have the luxury of selecting who your clients will be. Most of the time, they become the luck of the draw. Knowing how to use legal technicalities is an artful skill that works to the advantage of the Defense where an almost hopeless case can be resolved. Remember everyone has the right to a reasonable defense.*

---

I learned quite a bit about the state court system and met many prominent people while working at the Supreme Court. In particular, I befriended a state senator by the name of Don Bishop whose state office was located near the judicial center. His senatorial district was located in Oakland County. We became good friends. After many lunches at the Greek restaurant down the street and around the corner, the senator suggested I move to the small town of Rochester and join him in the practice of law, when my one-year commitment to the Supreme Court concluded. All the cards fell together fairly well and I moved to Rochester and set up my law practice in a spare office very close to the senator's office.

The Monday after returning from my honeymoon, I inaugurated my first law firm in a rented 500 sq. ft. office in downtown Rochester. To make my first impression on the business folks in my new town, I arrived at the local coffee shop at 8 am. After saying hello to all there and consuming a cup of coffee, I walked across the street with one of the city fathers. Neil Hartwig was a popular longtime real estate agent. His office was situated in a desirable location, a converted house positioned on the main corner downtown. As we crossed the street towards his office he said, "It is good to have a young Irish-Catholic lawyer in town. I will make sure to send some business your way. Welcome to the community." After eleven years and some months of practicing law down the street, not one client was referred to my office by Neil Hartwig. So much for quickly becoming a local; yet every time I ran into Neil at a public civic function, he was cheerful and most gratuitous. It is tough starting out in someone else's town.

From the beginning, I received most of my work through the circuit court public defender system. A call came into the office from the Assignment Clerk's office that I was assigned to handle the defense of Jay Seres. Seres was charged with Armed Robbery, a lifetime offense. He was accused of robbing a roadhouse bar on South Street in Rochester Hills. It turns out his MO (*modus operando*) was to enter the tavern around closing time, sit at the end of the bar and order a beer.

After pouring the last of the beer into his glass, Seres pointed the empty bottle, with a napkin draped over it, at the barkeeper and announced the stick-up. No mask, no gun, Seres was bold as brass right out in the open.

The next day, I received a notice of another assignment. The prosecutor added two new Armed Robbery charges against Seres and I was also asked to handle them. My first thought was to call the assistant prosecutors assigned to these cases to tell them to stop writing new charges. I was new to the game, but if they thought I could beat them on three armed robberies, I probably had quite a two-day reputation as a defense attorney. I drove over to the county jail later that day to see my client. Jay Seres was a large man with sort of a pleasant disposition. After a short conversation with him though, I could detect the ruthless mean streak hiding in there.

Seres was as street smart as any client I ever represented. He knew the system. He knew what I was supposed to do before I told him. He knew where he was heading, so it was up to both of us to obtain the best terms and conditions for his trip. I met with the prosecutor on the case at the pre-trial hearing. Most judges like to have the attorneys into their chambers so they can participate in the plea bargain process. The assistant prosecutor had other things on her mind that day and offered me a one-for-two. Seres would plead to one of the robberies and she would drop the two other counts. They always say, never accept the first offer. I partially agreed to the plea bargain, but I injected a maximum sentence of five years in prison. Something else must have been more important, because she agreed to these terms without quibbling. We had a deal. I now had to sell it to my client.

Court appointed counsel are paid very little according to a pay schedule in the circuit court administrator's office. The more serious the criminal offense, the greater the amount on the pay schedule. Seres had three life maximum charges hanging over his head. A jury trial on those three charges would pay substantially more than resolving the case with a plea bargain. By negotiating a plea arrangement with the assistant prosecutor was tantamount to negotiating a lower fee for the defense of the case. By now the deputy sheriffs guarding the courtroom knew that Jay Seres was one bad customer. He stood in the jury box with his hands and legs shackled while Judge Templin imposed the agreed upon sentence. Finally hearing his sentence of five years, Seres was very pleased because he knew he could be paroled after three years of good behavior. He quickly raised his chained hands to thank me. The deputies rushed to his side to protect me from possible injury. I looked back and told Jay to take care of himself.

*****

I rarely had walk-in clients mainly because my office was located in a professional office building. Clients were referred to me over the phone and we would schedule specific appointments to meet at the office. Peggy ran the office and she was as good as they get. Working with Peggy for a few years, I understood the phrase "right hand." Peggy was more than that; she was two times my right hand. This was back in the days of the IBM Selectric typewriters. One day an IBM salesman visited and suggested I upgrade my office equipment from the old Selectric to a first generation word processor. I told him I already had a word processor. It was Peggy.

Another day I called my office from circuit court to see if there were any messages I could handle while still on the road. Peggy said we had a walk-in client. She set a time when she knew I would be back in the office and asked him to return at 4pm that day. My new client returned on time and I met Mr. Walter Kasmerik for the first time. He was pinched for OUIL, operating under the influence of liquor. Walter lived in a small rural town of Capac, Michigan. He lived on a farm that used to be worked by his father. Every day Walter drove in to Rochester Hills to work at National Twist Drill Company. Walter was 36 years old and he had worked at Twist Drill for twelve years. The night he was arrested, he and his work buddies found their way to a local tavern for a little happy hour conversation. Needless to say, Walter stayed too long.

To get home from work every day, it was necessary for Walter to drive 6 miles north on Rochester Road, then 10 miles east on Romeo Road and then 20 further miles north on Van Dyke Road. That is a lot of driving exposure to law enforcement after partying with the boys. This evening Walter got no further than the Village of Romeo, where he was arrested by a trooper of the Michigan State Police. The state police regional post was located just north of the main intersection. The troopers keep a close eye on drivers traveling through town, right where Walter was placed under arrest.

Drunken driving cases are fairly predictable and often times turn out to become two separate cases. In addition to the criminal driving offense, the department of motor vehicles regularly suspends the driving privileges of those arrested until there is some disposition of the principle case. Because of court backloads, I was able to obtain an administrative hearing sooner in front of the regional representative of the Secretary of State to regain Walter's license. His arrest was the second week of December so I scheduled his driving hearing for the second week in January. After advising Walter of our schedule, I also told him I would be out of town for the holidays and cautioned him not to drink and not to drive while I was gone.

Our family always traveled to my wife's family home the week after Christmas and returned to the office the first week of January. The staff received a phone call from Walter Kasmerik my first day back in the office. I took the call and Walter said, "Mr. Sheee... Mr. Sheehy? I got arrested again by the sheriffs the other night." I ask him if he had been drinking. He told me that he was at home on the farm New Year's Eve. He had a few drinks and ran out of cigarettes. He just wanted to drive into the store to buy some smokes. Walter was arrested by two deputies from the St. Clair County sheriff's patrol for drunken driving. This made it two in a row...Great! I knew Walter was a loose cannon and his fees were starting to pile up.

I filed my appearance in two courts located in two different counties. That was followed with written requests for two Secretary of State (SOS) license restoration hearings. The first SOS hearing took place in Warren, in the southern part of Macomb County. Walter and I were present when the hearing officer called our case. To my amazement the arresting trooper failed to appear for the hearing. This was an easy dismissal and Walter's suspension on this portion of his driver's license was reinstated. It was a shallow victory, but a victory none the less. The second SOS hearing took place in a small office in the town of Marysville, located in St. Clair County. Testimony was taken from the two deputy sheriffs who arrested

Walter. They were watching a quiet desolate intersection surrounded by cornfields when they say Walter drove by them at a high rate of speed. They asked Walter to take a preliminary breath test in the parking lot of the beer and wine store, where he went to buy cigarettes. He blew a .14 and was arrested. Both deputies agreed they failed to advise Walter of his right to refuse the breath test at the sheriff's lock-up or his right to this SOS hearing. That was all I needed, a technical glitch in the mandatory police procedure. By the end of this hearing, I was able to persuade the hearing officer to return and restore Walter's driver's license. The score was two down and two to go.

Now for something a little more complicated. I had asked for jury trials on both of the criminal drunk driving cases. My goal was to find one or two sympathetic drinkers as jurors and plead my case to them. We arrived at the appointed hour in the Romeo court for jury selection on the first OUIL case. Judge McLean had been on the bench in that court since the inauguration of the District Court system in 1969. We became friends on a previous drinking and driving case. That client then was the father of eight and I asked the judge for leniency because of that fact. Judge McLean quickly countered to me, "What else can your client do?" After sitting around most of the day waiting to select a jury, the assistant prosecutor came out of his office and advised me that the arresting trooper had been transferred by the state police to a post in the

Upper Peninsula (the U-P) and he would be unavailable to participate in the trial. I immediately asked the judge to dismiss this case with prejudice and he did just that. You never want to leave a matter like this open, just in case the trooper is transferred back.

The next of Walter's trials was not going to be as easy. A jury was selected in a small courtroom on the second floor of the county courthouse in downtown Port Huron. This was my first time trying anything before the Honorable Wilber Hamm, District Judge. The trial did not take long. The same two deputies testified to the same facts as they did at the license restoration hearing. The first deputy was the tough macho guy. He was very assured of what he saw the evening of the arrest with his unwavering testimony. He said that he and his partner had been together as a one-car team for twelve years. I asked him how many drunken driving arrests they made over those years and if every driver was really drunk. He answered that they made hundreds of alcohol related stops and yes, they were all drunk. The first deputy left the courtroom and the second sequestered deputy arrived to testify. He was not present in court to hear his partner's testimony so I asked him the same questions. The second deputy was not as sure of himself about how the events of the evening transpired. My cross examination was focused on trying to compare and contrast the factual differences testified to by each deputy. I asked him if they ever made any alcohol arrests in the past twelve years. He explained that he and his partner were rural patrol officers and the made fewer than twenty arrests over that period. I accidentally found something I could talk to the jury about. Because of the technical errors of the deputies on the night of the arrest, the breath/alcohol values from Walter's breath test were not admitted into the trial for the jury to consider. The assistant prosecutor argued that this case was a slam dunk and the jury should find Walter guilty of drunk driving. Now it was my turn to persuade the jury with closing argument. I itemized all the conflicts in the testimony of the deputies. They were working together for twelve years and one made hundreds of alcohol stops and the other made less than twenty arrests. One deputy was so sure the driver sped and smelled like alcohol and the other was not as sure. "Ladies and Gentlemen of the Jury, how much of the deputies' testimony can you believe?" I said. The answer was clear, "None of it!"

Judge Hamm quickly excused the jury with his only admonition to go back to the jury room and find Walter guilty or not-guilty. I had never heard a judge charge a jury like that. After the jury was sequestered out of the earshot of the courtroom, I asked the judge to return the jury and charge them in accordance to the standard jury instructions for a case such as this. I had a copy of the official jury instructions approved by the Michigan Supreme Court with me. With a grand wave of his hand, Judge Hamm denied my request and said they know why they are here and they can figure out what to do by themselves. His comments were astonishing. This was not just a clerical error reminiscent of the deputies' failure to advise Walter of his rights on the night of the arrest. This was a fatal error by the trial judge. Any way this case was decided by the jury, I knew now I had a reversal in my pocket with a Circuit Court appeal. Two hours later, the jury returned to the courtroom to announce their verdict. "Not Guilty," they declared. I thanked everybody and quickly found my car in the parking lot. I had spent more than enough time in Port Huron with Walter.

Walter became a no-show in my office for two weeks, so I gave him a call to see how he was doing. He still owed me $400 on his $1200 fee (pretty cheap at today's prices) and I did not want him to forget about it. Later that day Walter walked in and made his final payment. He never offered me a thank you for winning four different court appearances. That is gratitude, I thought, but turned around and walked out the office door. That was the last time I saw Walter Kasmerik

Later that year, a radio station reported a prison break from the maximum security Marquette Prison in the Upper Peninsula. A couple of inmates got loose and were believed to be heading down the Wisconsin coast towards Chicago. I did not give it a moment of thought at that time. Arriving at court two days later, the talk around the building was that an Oakland County deputy sheriff had been shot on the third shift the night before. I knew who the deputy was from seeing him in court, so I asked for more facts.

The deputy stopped a fleeing car on a gravel road on the east side of town. The driver got out with a shot gun in his hand and fired one round at the deputy. The deputy protected himself by standing behind his open patrol car door. One-errant buckshot from a burst ricocheted off the door and hit the deputy in the eye affecting his eyesight. Within a half hour it seemed, every police car in the county arrived to surround the assailant holed up in a vacant house on South Street. Dogs were called in and a standoff ensued for more than an hour. The police then heard a muffled gunshot sound coming from inside the hemmed-in house. After a short time with no further contact, they carefully entered the vacant building and found the lifeless body of Jay Seres—dead from a self-inflicted gunshot wound. Yes, he was the same Jay Seres who had escaped from Marquette a couple of days earlier.

*****

As a municipal attorney it was necessary to practice administrative law in the state regulatory departments. Neighboring cities annexed away areas from the Township of Pontiac just for the purpose of building garbage landfills to service their citizen's needs. Finally we rewrote the township charter to insure there would be no further annexations by any adjoining community.

On the north side of the township, a disposal site of waste material had been constructed long before the city became incorporated. A commercial landfill must be constructed in accordance with explicit engineering specifications. The Lapeer Road Dump landfill was not properly designed according to present day law. In the year of 1974, the Federal government required all landfills be lined with a rubberized landfill liner to prevent contamination by leachates migrating downward through the underlying geological formation. The bottom of any landfill must also be lined with a thick layer of clay, so that any decomposition does not leak or leach out in the form of toxic liquids. Large cities like the City of Detroit dispose of 80% of their garbage and refuse into landfills. And most of the garbage hauled to the Lapeer Road Dump daily by the J. Fons Company was from the City of Detroit. After years of over utilization, the half mile square Lapeer Road Dump was seriously decaying and sending real nasty liquid materials into the underground aquifers. The fresh trout streams that flowed through the area were becoming affected. The Michigan Department of Natural Resources is the only group that has the last word as to closing down this unnatural man-made disaster.

The township officials decided that poisoning of the neighborhoods around the dump had to be stopped. We filed a petition to have the dump closed. The State of Michigan issued a preliminary cease and desist order from an administrative judge. Sixty days later, the Supervisor Bob Grusnick and I drove up to the capital city for a full hearing on how the toxic poisons were leaching into the community's water supply. I treated this hearing in front of an administrative judge as any other trial and subpoenaed expert witnesses to testify in the small makeshift courtroom at the state capital. We told the administrative judge how the Lapeer Road Dump was one of the worst ecological problems in the state. The judge said an opinion would be issued in the near future.

Two weeks later the word reached the supervisor's office that the Lapeer Road Dump was officially and permanently closed for any further landfill activity by the state authorities. That dump never reopened, to my amazement. Venting tubes spouting flames continuously burned off the gaseous methane residues for the next twenty years. Everyone could see those flickering candles in the dark of night from miles away. Years later after leaving the City of Auburn Hill for the bench, a new garbage landfill was correctly constructed across the street on Lapeer Road to support the continuous large deliveries of garbage and refuse from Detroit. As the mounds of garbage grew taller and taller creating a small mountain, I renamed the site after our supervisor/mayor to Mount Grusnick.

**And then there is this...**

Never turn down an invitation to play a round of golf. You can by no means tell what it will lead to. When opportunity stares you in the face, grab it.

After three years of working full time and attending law school full time, my education drew to a close. In reality, however, we never stop learning through attending lectures, seminars and workshops. A good friend and classmate Fred Schultz approached me after the completion of our senior year final exams and asked if I would be attending the Gamma Outing the next week. Unaware of the event, an explanation was in order. Fred said it was an end-of-year golf outing put on by one of the legal fraternities. I told Fred I did not play golf and, to be sure, I may have played around; but I had never played a round of golf. I only watched from outside the fences. Not once did I have the time or the inclination for that sport.

Fred really wanted me to join in so he sweetened his request by giving me a set of his old clubs if I appeared at the school closing event. I asked if there was a dinner reception and a social bar. Yes, in fact it would be an open bar. I was all in on this one.

Now my first attempt at the golf game was nothing to talk about. The score was well over 100 and a dozen or so balls stayed on the course. The "social" part couldn't come soon enough. A large group was present enjoying

"Happy Hour", including acquaintances who had graduated from the law school in the past few years. I ran across Mike Devine who I was surprised to find was now Chief of Staff for the Chief Justice of the Michigan Supreme Court.

After some small talk, Mike asked where I intended to open my practice of law. I was currently employed with Michigan Mutual Insurance Company as a claims adjuster and had hoped to find a spot in their legal department. He said his office was looking to fill a clerk's position and would I be interested? "Grab it," I thought. Sure, Mike!

Within a week I interviewed and was hired as a law clerk to the best boss I ever had, the Honorable Thomas E. Brennan, Chief Justice. And that my friend is why you never turn down an invitation to play a round of golf.

# Chapter Four

# B & E Boys

*Some of the south end cops had their watchful surveillance eye on the pool hall Joe's dad used for his bookmaking operation. One second shift cop, now forced to work days on this special pool hall detail, started to catch on to the daily routine after casing the joint for a couple of weeks. Joe's dad drove to work in an old maroon 1955 Mercury that had lost the luster of the original paint because of the acid rain from the steel mill smoke stacks in the neighborhood. Following the last horse race every day, he would gather up all his betting slips, place them in the right-rear tire rim of his car, and secure them under the hubcap. The big palooka cop set his eyes on taking him down. One day, after Joe's dad secured the daily work product under the hubcap, he went back inside to find his overcoat. For that brief moment, stepping into the pool hall and back to his car, the cop snuck up to the ugly Mercury and loosened the right-rear hubcap. As Joe's dad pulled away from the curb, that hubcap fell off the wheel and all the secured betting slips fell into the gutter; easy pickings for the waiting vice cop.*

*The next week the cop charged Joe's dad with five felony counts of violating the gambling laws. This cop never cared for what he sensed was the special treatment some criminal defendants received because of liberal constitutional rights. The cop thought, by golly, the bookie was collared fair and square, so why not throw the book at him. He seemed a little short on the sensitivity one might find in a more seasoned member of his department. On the other hand, Joe's dad knew he had to defend himself in pro per, as they say, because he could not afford his own attorney.*
*To be continued...*

---

Everybody has the right to representation by an attorney, especially if you are unable to afford to hire your own. No one told that to Joe's dad.

Each circuit judge assigned public defender lawyers to their allocated cases. They keep their own list of attorneys they think are capable of handling a specific criminal case. Clearly, there were no criteria, at the time, as to whose name would get picked from which judges' defender list. It took on the qualities of the "good old boy system." On my very first day of private practice, I drove over to the county courthouse to introduce myself to the various judges working at that time and to their secretaries. I quickly realized the secret to the appointment system—getting to know each judge's secretary. Judge Clark Adams, a former Supreme Court justice, returned to his home county to continue his judicial career on the county circuit court bench. He did not appreciate I was recently on the Supreme Court staff or that this case was my first criminal assignment with his court. We just seemed to naturally get along with each other, right from the start. The judge said to his secretary, "Let the kid handle this case." Later when Judge Adams realized my past employer, we became even closer friends. Another important component about the practice of law is being careful with whom you do business and be cautious with whom you associate. I learned this was true during all my years of practicing law.

Two local young men were itching to take someone else's property, so they broke into a residential home on Huron Street to satisfy that urge. This was back in the days when the police shot first and asked questions later. The burglars tripped the silent home alarm that went directly to police headquarters and a squad car was rapidly dispatched and quickly descended upon the residence. Police vehicles are sometimes called "rollers or "black and whites"; often times they are followed to the crime scene by "black marias" or "paddy wagons", slang terms for police vans used to transport prisoners.

The looters escaped through the back window of the home as soon as they saw the police arrive. The cops rounded the corner of the house with their guns drawn and shot one of them in the leg, before he was able to reach the alleyway. The police took him over to the hospital a few blocks away, patched him up and then lodged him into the county sheriff's main jail. His partner and soon to be co-defendant was observed and arrested on a side-street before he could reach his home. He, too, quickly arrived at the county jail.

The prosecutor charged these B&E boys with Breaking and Entering an Occupied Dwelling House. A dwelling house is termed *occupied* if someone lives in the house, whether or not present at home during the robbery. If no one lives in the house, the charge would read *unoccupied*. Today these types of charges are known as Home Invasion.

I thought a good place to start preparing this criminal case was at the central police station, where I dropped by and looked around, having never been there before. I asked for the detective bureau and introduced myself to the detective-in-charge of the case of the two bad boys. After some small chitchat by way of introduction, the detective gave me a copy of the police report of the facts involved in their investigation. I read the write-up and returned it to the detective. At this point, I thought I had a pretty good idea of what happened at the crime scene.

The court date for the preliminary hearing was a few days away, so I decided to drive over to the county jail and pay a visit to at least one of the B&E boys. I first visited the wounded defendant, the one shot in the leg near the alleyway. After introducing myself, I told him Judge Adams appointed me to represent him on the Home Invasion charge. He interrupted, "Why am I locked up, I ain't done nothin at all. I was just walking down the damn alley when that trigger-happy cop came out and shot me. Can't you do nuthin about that? Can't we sue those bastards for what they done?" he asked. I paused and listened to his story, which sounded much different from the facts I read in the police write up. "I'll be able to better tell you what is going on if you have the right answer to one question ... OK?" I asked.

"Do you remember the earrings the police found in your pocket when they arrested you?" He answered, "Yea man, dem belonged to my girlfriend."

I continued, "Well, the escape window was broken out and sitting on the inside of the window sill was a full necklace that matched those earrings. Can you explain to me how your girlfriend's necklace got inside that house?" With that question there was dead silence, accompanied with the longest stare. Finally, he asked, "O.K. what kind of deal can you do for me? What can you get?"

My case research was over. When we got to court the next day or so, I advised the court there was no need to take testimony, "My clients wish to waive their rights to a preliminary examination and have this matter bound over to circuit court where it will be resolved with some sort of a plea."

Criminal pre-trials usually take place at the same hearing where the defendants are formally arraigned, called the Arraignment on the Information. With the charges acknowledged in open court, a negotiated plea may be entered. A recent increase of felony arrests countywide had caused the county jail overcrowding, so the prosecutor agreed to reduce the charge to an Attempted Breaking and Entering, which would reduce the maximum sentence to five years in prison and move the B&E boys out of the county jail immediately. They both agreed to enter a plea of guilty to the attempted charge and receive a sentence of three to five years in the state prison. A parole hearing is available after serving 80% of the minimum sentence. They thanked me for my representation, smiled and walked out of the court directly into the detention center bus for an afternoon ride to prison. The plea negotiation process looks very easy, especially in this case, but I knew the judge, the prosecutor and the detectives. All the parties agreed on the outcome in this case, but negotiations do not always come to pass that way.

*****

A practicing lawyer has many responsibilities, clearly laid out in the State's Code of Professional Responsibility. A lawyer, as an officer of the legal system, has a special responsibility for the quality of justice. He or she plays the role of an advisor to clients, an advocate of their legal position, an evaluator of their legal rights and obligations and a mediator of conflicts among differing positions. The lawyer must be competent and diligent in the performance of these roles. He or she is a professional who gives their full respect for all those in the legal system. "A lawyer should strive to attain the highest level of skill, to improve the law and the legal profession and to exemplify the legal profession's ideals of public service." (Michigan Code of Professional Responsibility)

Sometimes a lawyer's responsibility to his client's interests conflicts with his professional responsibility to conduct himself in the highest ethical manner and abide by the rules that govern his conduct. The Rules of Professional Conduct provide the means for resolving these conflicts. "Lawyers play a vital role in the preservation of society. The fulfillment of this role requires an understanding by the lawyers of their relationship to our legal system. The Rules of Professional Conduct, when properly applied, serve to define that relationship."

The following actions by public officials clearly demonstrate where the lawyers involved did not properly handle conflicts with their legal and professional duties.

Kwame Kilpatrick, mayor of the City of Detroit and his chief of staff committed perjury, false testimony under oath, in the defense of a civil trial against the city. The perjured testimony, of which they were later convicted, was an effort to cover up their personal romantic affair. The mayor was a lawyer and the staff chief was a law student. Law students, as well as everyone else, are obliged to follow the law and testify to the truth while under oath. Each of the lawyers representing them in the original trial also participated in the cover-up, which is by definition suborning perjury, a serious criminal offense. The mayor was later disbarred from the practice of law, the law student was not allowed to take the bar exam or practice law and their two lawyers were suspended from the practice of law by the State Bar Grievance Board for a period of years.

In another case, an assistant prosecutor requested Judge Waterstone, a circuit judge to allow an undercover officer to lie while testifying in open court about certain pertinent facts in a criminal drug trial. The judge granted the request and the fact that the witness was a paid snitch, was not divulged in the trial. When the cover-up became known to the public about the judge allowing perjured testimony, the judge voluntarily retired in an attempt to avoid a felony charge. The chief assistant prosecutor lost her job and was charged with felonies in the nature of obstructing justice. None of the above would have taken place had each public official properly followed their respective Rules of Professional Conduct.

The judge, the assistant prosecutor and the two police officers involved in the cover-up received minimum sentences upon their convictions.

# Chapter Five

# Malevolent Prosecutions

*The trial day came and Joe's dad walked alone into the courtroom of The Honorable John Gillis., referred to by some lawyers as "Old Judge Gillis." He had no idea of what was going on or what was to follow. He stood before the court without a lawyer by his side and was overwhelmed by his going-it-alone anxiety. This is usually the case when one has never been in a courtroom.*

*Any judge worth his salt tries to resolve a case before having to impanel a jury, which could take the better part of an entire day. The confident cop with all his court experience and the tough-on-crime prosecutor stood shoulder to shoulder to the right of the judge and Joe's dad insignificantly stood to the left in front of good Old Judge Gillis.*

*The judge first addressed the prosecutor. "Mr. Prosecutor, have you tried to settle this matter with the defendant? Have you made him a plea offer for consideration?" The prosecutor quickly responded. "No your honor, the officer tells me he's has this guy cold on all the counts and he wants to take it all the way today." He then mumbled something about organized crime.*

*The judge thanked him and slowly turned his overstuffed chair towards Joe's dad and said in a conciliatory tone, "Do you have anything to say for yourself before we begin this trial?" All he could think of saying was, "Well your honor, I live in the northwest side of town. I have never been involved with the law. I have three children who attend St. Elizabeth's grade school. I am a member of the St. Elizabeth's Usher Club and a sustaining member of the Ancient Order of the Hibernians." His knees were really trembling by this time. Judge Gillis did not hesitate. He slapped his bench and said; "Now we have something to talk about. You don't look as guilty now as I first thought you did."*

*By the end of the session and after hours of plea-bargaining discussions, the judge took under advisement all the charges and Joe's dad drove home, as if he was returning from another day at the pool hall. Ten months later, the Court expunged the arrest record when dad promised to stop taking bets. By the way, Judge Gillis was honored by the metropolitan Hibernian group, an Irish-Catholic men's group, and only two weeks previous to this case coming to court.*

---

When entertainer Jerry Lewis began to broadcast nationwide his telethon to raise money to combat all forms of Muscular Dystrophy, kids around the country contributed to the cause by means of organized car washes and bake sales. McDonald franchisees collaborated with the fundraisers to make larger contributions. Firemen stood up before studio cameras dressed in their simple, but identifiable, uniforms making their donations. We were proud of them for their public involvement. Our community pride allowed us, in some respect, to share their participation in the cause. We always look for heroes. We look for leaders we may possibly admire. Our dads and moms loved us and were true to us.

Ministers and priests formed our spiritual belief of the good in this world and the principle that good things happen to good people. We were told, "The policeman is your friend." They are always there to protect us from the bad guys. Mayors and city council persons have the responsibility of leadership for the greater good of the community. The judges and prosecutors are on our side, just like the police, to protect the whole community from awful things happening. At least that is what it seemed to be while growing up. We conduct our lives in the same way were raised, while maturing into adulthood. With the help of experience and knowledge, the veneer slowly begins to crack and peal back. Now we look at real life, without those rose colored glasses.

*****

The last case I handled as a lawyer, before becoming a judge, was defending a township deputy treasurer charged with embezzlement of public funds. Dorothy Sites was a middle-aged, single parent who worked at the Orion Township Hall for quite a few years. The annual auditors found funds in two special water department accounts missing. Dorothy was charged with stealing those missing monies. I had developed a habit of never asking the defendants I represented whether or not they committed a crime or if they were guilty of the offense with which they were charged. That type of information cluttered up the defense process with all sorts of emotional drama that always seemed to get in the way of making clear decisions.

The township fired Dorothy immediately with no discussions. I demanded they have a due process hearing to obtain more information of the alleged crime which necessitated filing a Federal Court lawsuit to obtain those rights. Herma Snyder, associate editor of the *Oxford-Orion Times,* was present in the council chambers and reported on what she saw at the hearing.

"It was a moving and educational experience, the due process hearing for Dorothy Sites at the Orion Township Hall. ... I couldn't help but agree with James Sheehy, Sites attorney, that the matter seemed more serious than an ordinary dismissal. I think he did a marvelous job of reminding everyone that a person is presumed innocent until proven guilty. Like everyone else, I kept staring at Dorothy Sites—as though a closer look could see into the truth of this affair. But what I saw was an attractive woman, who sat demurely and silently at the side of her attorney.

"Sheehy ran the gamut of emotions from aggravated tolerance, disbelief, incredibility, warmth and understanding. He doesn't look too impressive, with thinning hair and a mustache and rather unpressed trousers. When he began to speak, I even thought he was a little too antagonistic, protesting this, that and everything.

"Summing it up, I guess I'm trying to say that I found James Sheehy a refreshing experience. He reminded us all that strange, bizarre things happen—that what seems to be is not necessarily what is—and that life is sometimes stranger than fiction.

"Despite my tendency to jump to matter-of-fact conclusions, despite my feeling there is a direct path to a given point—I left the hearing glad there is an attorney like James Sheehy in the world and that the laws of the country guarantee every one of us a moment of truth."

Prosecutors are required by law to divulge all the police information, facts from any investigation and all the names of witnesses and furnish that information to the defense attorney before the trial date; *Brady v. Maryland,* called it the Brady Rule. An attorney from the state's attorney general's office in the capital city was assigned to prosecute the Sites case. No attorney or judge from this county knew of him or how he conducted his business. Adding to the confusion, I was required to turn over this case just before trial to another attorney, because of my judicial conflict. I asked Professor Keenan, my longtime friend, to step into my shoes and try the case, during his summer recess from the law school. Pat tried the fairly uncomplicated criminal lawsuit. During the trial, however, Pat found out there were other witnesses that may have benefited Dorothy at trial. These types of witnesses are called exculpatory witnesses. The prosecutor is also required to turn over to the defense attorney the names of the exculpatory witnesses and not hide them from the defense. Nondisclosure of information and witnesses' names is favorite little trick of inexperienced assistant prosecutors who believe they must win their cases at any cost. Unfortunately such behavior is unethical and reversible error, if caught in the act.

Dorothy was convicted by the jury and sentenced by Judge George LaPlata to a year and a day in the women's prison. The judge's friends in the bar association always referred to Judge LaPlata by his nickname, "Chico". He seemed to be upset that he needed to hold this trial and took it out on Dorothy with a stiff and immediate sentence.

Not long after Dorothy was sentenced and dragged off to prison, Keenan appealed the conviction on the grounds of prosecutorial misconduct, which took one and a half years until the Court of Appeals could hear the case.

From the Appeals Court opinion, they said this about her trial:

"Defendant was not provided with certain items covered by the discovery order until mid-trial. Defendant claims such action by the prosecution was contrary to said order and prejudice resulted from such untimely disclosure. We agree and REVERSE.

"In *People v Pace*, 102 Mich App 522, (1980), this Court held:

> 'Where a prosecutor has violated a discovery order, even if done inadvertently in good faith, unless it is clear that the failure to divulge was harmless beyond a reasonable doubt, we will reverse.'

"Applying this test to the case at bar, we find first that the prosecutor violated a discovery order by failing to timely disclose certain information to defense counsel. In spite of defendant's repeated demands and the court's order for disclosure of all witnesses' statements, a tape recorded statement of William Morris taken two months prior to defendant being charged was not turned over to defense counsel until the third day of trial. Additionally, the prosecution refused to disclose certain notes of Detective Wood's interviews with 50 Orion Township residents and it was not until the fourth day of trial that defense counsel was afforded an opportunity to examine the notes of 23 of said interviews. Both items were clearly subject to the discovery order and failure to timely disclosure was a violation thereof.

"Next, under *Pace*, we must ascertain if the violation of the discovery order was harmless beyond a reasonable doubt. On the tape, Morris described defendant a 'dark' haired, not a 'blond'. This contradicts the defendant's actual appearance. In addition, Morris stated that defendant 'didn't look anything like this picture (on the employee I.D. card) you showed me.'

"Finally, Morris said, 'but I couldn't just go somewhere and swear it was her.' Identification of defendant is crucial to this case. The tape is exculpatory in that it indicates Morris could not positively identify defendant. Defendant should have been provided with the tape before mid-trial. We hold that failure to disclose the tape prejudiced the defendant and was not harmless beyond a reasonable doubt.

"The prosecutor's failure to timely disclose the notes of the interviews with 50 Orion residents also resulted in prejudice to the defendant. Several residents reported that they made payments to people who did not meet defendant's description. For example, Loretta Weaver described the person she paid as 'tall, slender girl 23, 30 years, five-ten, dark hair.' This description does not fit defendant. These reports contradict the prosecutor's contention that defendant had virtually complete control of all monies going through the office and almost always received the payments herself. Defense counsel unsuccessfully attempted to contact several of these residents during trial. Had the prosecution given timely disclosure, all interviewees could have been interviewed by defense counsel and been subpoenaed prior to trial. Timely disclosure was especially crucial with respect to Loretta Weaver since she died prior to trial."

By that time Dorothy completed her sentence and was out of prison and back home, the Court of Appeals reversed the case and sent it back to the circuit court for a new trial, but there would be no new trial. Since Dorothy completed her sentence, she could no longer be re-tried and re-sentenced a second time for the same offense. Dorothy's criminal conviction was wiped off her public record. Professor Keenan thought about having her fingerprint cards returned, but he became too busy teaching at the law school and unable to find the time. It was hard to believe, I thought, that prosecutorial misconduct took place in the case I prepared for trial. The only thing I could do now as a judge was to keep a watchful eye on the way each assistant prosecutor behaved while they were in my courtroom.

*****

In 2006, a group of lacrosse players from Duke University in Durham, North Carolina organized a private party at which a couple of dancers participated as the entertainment. Afterwards one of the dancers, a black woman, complained to the police she had been raped at the party. The county district attorney took the police report to the grand jury and three lacrosse players were indicted on charges of kidnapping and rape. Michael Byron Nifong, the district attorney for Durham County was facing election later that year to retain his office. Nifong was initially supported by the Duke faculty and administration along with feminist minority groups for taking this strong position on behalf of the black dancer against the white students. The case also became a racial *cause célébré*. Nifong's critics called this a political publicity stunt to give support to his election efforts.

The young students denied any contact with the complaining stripper and cooperated with the police in their investigation. Duke University, the public media and Nifong strongly went public condemning the students. The prosecutor was mistakenly encouraged by the editorial support he received from *The New York Times*. Nifong made comments meant to enrage racial tensions, while he stifled the police participation in the case. He overtly tried to manipulate the words of witnesses. After six months of trying the case in the press, Nifong still had never interviewed the complaining witness. With all the public attention, the one complaining witness began to change her story and denied being raped. The tide began to turn on Prosecutor Nifong. The North Carolina citizenry became enraged in the local prosecutor's behavior. The maligned prosecutor turned the case over to the state's attorney general for handling. After the attorney general completed his investigation into the complaints of the dancers, he dismissed all the criminal proceedings for lack of evidence. The attorney general referred to Nifong as "a rogue prosecutor." Even though Nifong won election the following November, he was promptly taken before the state's attorney grievance board to answer the complaints about the way he handled this case. The newly elected prosecutor was summarily disbarred from any further practice of law, because of his prosecutorial misconduct. It seemed to me that this was the most overt abuse of the power by a prosecutor I ever witnessed, up to that point in time.

*****

In 1978, Terry Harrington and Curtis McGhee were convicted of first-degree murder by the State of Iowa based on manufactured evidence and failure to disclose exculpatory evidence. They each served twenty-five years in prison, before being released by a current prosecutor. Here is what happened. I will try to make it simple. A night security guard who was a retired police officer was shot to death while protecting an auto dealership in Council Bluffs, Iowa. Two city detectives led the murder investigation. An assistant county attorney became intensely involved in the investigation, even though his office had not sanctioned him to get involved. A witness positively identified a man with a dog and a shotgun at the murder scene, shortly before the shooting. The police knew him to be Donald Gates.

The police, however, turned their attention to a sixteen year old with a long criminal record and pressed him for information about a possible killer. They promised Kevin Hughes that he would not be charged in this case with murdering the guard. Hughes had current charges pending and the police promised to clear them and Hughes would be given a $5,000 reward for his testimony. The detectives and assistant county attorney named Hrvol put pressure on Hughes to implicate Harrington and McGhee. The police and Hrvol supplied information about the murder weapon to Hughes and used him as their chief witness to convict Harrington and McGhee. The prosecutor failed to inform the defense attorneys about the dozen persons under investigation. Hrvol lied when he said they were never able to identify the "man with the dog and shotgun". Hughes and the other juvenile witnesses used at trial later recanted their sworn testimonies and said they lied in order to obtain the cash reward.

Harrington and McGhee were released through the efforts of a prison employee who conducted her own independent investigation. Harrington and McGhee brought civil rights actions against the county and the former prosecutors involved in the initial investigation, for using perjured and fabricated testimony and for withholding evidence from the defense in violation of their constitutional rights. The prosecutor did not deny his legal wrongdoing. He stood, however, behind the shield of immunity; claiming he was immune from any legal responsibility and damages because of his position as a public official at the time. There is only one word I can think fits this situation: *Incomprehensible.*

Harrington and McGhee spent twenty-five years, a lifetime, in jail because the prosecutor rigged the evidence. Now the prosecutor claims he cannot be held responsible for the unethical, illegal behavior and the wrongful conviction and incarceration. The Federal Appeals court agreed with Harrington and McGhee. Prosecutors, they say, have absolute immunity for performing distinctly prosecutorial functions. Obtaining, manufacturing, coercing and fabricating evidence before the filing of formal charges, however, is not a prosecutorial function and does not qualify for immunity.

This case was appealed to the United States Supreme Court and the *Washington Post* editorialized on giving prosecutors full immunity in this particular case.

"It is a breathtaking proposition that the justices should roundly reject when they hear the case...The vast majority of prosecutors perform honorably and understand that they are duty-bound not just to secure convictions, but also to seek justice. Those who don't often suffer any consequences at the hands of State or bar organizations, as a brief in support of Mr. McGhee and Mr. Harrington convincingly argued. For these few renegades, perhaps the prospect of being held liable will help to keep them in line or, at least, hold them accountable."

Unique to the appellate courts, interested parties are invited to present their positions on the points of law being considered by the court. These position papers, briefs or learned treatises are called *Amicus Curiae* briefs, which is Latin meaning Friend of the Court. Appellate cases are normally presented on the factual record and arguments. Where a case may have broader implications, *amicus curiae* briefs are a way to introduce concerns of outside groups and influence the outcome of the final opinion of the court.

In the *McGhee* case, there were no fewer than five national organizations that presented *amicus* briefs supporting the immunity of the public official. Two *amicus* briefs favored the plaintiffs' positions. The principle of absolute immunity for prosecutors from civil lawsuits and liability for their actions during trial was settled law by *Imber v. Pachtman* in 1976. Former Solicitor General Paul Clement took the position that the fabrication of perjured testimony against Harrington and McGhee violated their substantive due process rights to a fair trial. Clement contended prosecutorial misconduct that is "so ill-motivated as to shock the conscience" violates substantive due process whenever it occurs. In this case, the prosecutors' intent to use the perjured testimony at trial, regardless whether they ever presented it, demonstrates that they were in fact "ill-motivated." He went on to say it is necessary to deter prosecutorial misconduct; otherwise, "prosecutors would be free to fabricate evidence during criminal investigations because they would know there was virtually no possibility of ever being punished for it."

The National District Attorney's Association, the largest and primary professional association of prosecuting attorneys in the United States, took the following position in their *amicus* brief. "The doctrine of absolute immunity is intended to preclude the very real risk that prosecutors will face with civil lawsuits and potential liabilities imposed by civil damages over the conduct of their official duties and thereby chill prosecutorial efforts that are necessary to combat and deter crime. The increase of litigation will impose burdens on the prosecutors in terms of both time and money." Earlier I told you about the last case I handled before becoming a judge. In the Dorothy Sites case, the state's assistant attorney general failed to disclose the names of witnesses that could have helped her in the defense of the case. In my lifetime experiences, I found that failing to fully disclose all the evidence obtained in the police investigation by the prosecution voluntarily is not as unusual as it may seem.

Go off on a tangent with me for a moment and try to better understand this narrow-minded logic. Juxtapose the prosecutorial immunity proposition with the medical profession, if you will. The doctors deter and combat disease and death. They face the threat of civil lawsuits and civil damages every day from the conduct of their practice, when a patient walks into their office or when they operate in a hospital. It is undeniable these lawsuits place a chill on their efforts and cause doctors to order many unnecessary tests, often times to cover their own tracks. Doctors could, in a sense, be considered public employees, keeping in mind their relationship with Medicare and Medicaid and all the regulations controlling their practice. Doctors practice medicine without any immunity; and no one has yet to suggest granting them the same immunity for simple negligence given these public officials.

Immunity for negligent behavior of prosecutors is one thing, but intentional prosecutorial misconduct that is "so ill-motivated as to shock the conscience." is not acceptable behavior for any normal red-blooded person. In the end, the county government that employed prosecutors Richter and Hrvol agreed to pay Harrington and McGhee $12 million just days before the United States Supreme Court was to issue their opinion in this matter. The two men still have a lawsuit pending against the City of Council Bluffs and the police officers.

*****

John Thompson spent 14 years on death row because prosecutors concealed exculpatory blood evidence from his defense attorney. When Thompson was first tried in 1985, prosecutors in the Orleans Parish District Attorney's Office had strategically pursued the attempted robbery charge prior to the murder charge, to dissuade Thompson from testifying at his murder trial for fear of his criminal record being introduced to the jury. Prosecutors also neglected to inform Thompson's public defender that the perpetrator of the robbery had left his blood on the pants leg of one of the victims. A test performed on a swatch of fabric taken from the pants conclusively established that the perpetrator's blood was type B; Thompson's blood, which prosecutors never tested, is type O. Thompson's execution date was only weeks away when an investigator working for his defense team found an exculpatory blood-evidence report in an obscure file buried in the New Orleans Police Crime Laboratory. Years later, when Thompson was finally cleared of the robbery charge and free to testify on his own behalf, the jury at his retrial for murder acquitted him after only thirty-five minutes of deliberation.

After the discovery of the exculpatory evidence and his subsequent acquittal, Thompson sued Harry Connick, Sr., the District Attorney of Orleans Parish, alleging that Connick's deliberate indifference to an obvious need to train the prosecutors in his office caused the prosecutors' failure to turn over exculpatory evidence in Thompson's case. It became apparent from evidence presented at trial that Connick's office offered no formal training to its prosecutors regarding *Brady* type evidence. The jury awarded Thompson $14 million.

This case, *Connick v. Thompson*, was reversed by the United States Supreme Court on March 29, 2011. According to Justice Thomas's majority opinion, a single *Brady* violation—i.e., a one-time failure to disclose "material" evidence—is insufficient to establish liability on a failure-to-train theory.

The Yale Law Journal Online reported on the above case in an essay named:

**The Myth of Prosecutorial Accountability After Connick v. Thompson: Why Existing Professional Responsibility Measures Cannot Protect Against Prosecutorial**

The Project's review of the public disciplinary actions reported in the *California State Bar Journal*, however, revealed a mere six—out of a total of 4741—that involved prosecutorial misconduct. "What little evidence we do have indicates that prosecutorial misconduct is a serious problem. A 2003 study by the Center for Public Integrity, for instance, found over two thousand appellate cases since 1970 in which prosecutorial misconduct led to dismissals, sentence reductions, or reversals. Another study of all American capital convictions between 1973 and 1995 revealed that state post-conviction courts found "prosecutorial suppression of evidence that the defendant is innocent or does not deserve the death penalty" in one in six cases where the conviction was reversed. Other scholars and journalists have also documented widespread prosecutorial misconduct throughout the United States."

"Given the Supreme Court's repeated endorsement of professional discipline as the appropriate vehicle for addressing allegations of prosecutorial misconduct, one might suppose that state bar agencies frequently sanction prosecutors. In fact, prosecutors are rarely held accountable for violating ethics rules. In 1999, *Chicago Tribune* reporters Maurice Possley and Ken Armstrong identified 381 homicide cases nationally in which *Brady* violations produced conviction reversals. Not a single prosecutor in those cases was publicly sanctioned. Four years later, a study by the Center for Public Integrity found 2012 appellate cases between 1970 and 2003 in which prosecutorial misconduct led to dismissals, sentence reductions, or reversals. Yet prosecutors faced disciplinary action in only forty-four of those cases, and seven of these actions were eventually dismissed. The most recent study indicates that depressingly little has changed since 2003, at least in California. The Northern California Innocence Project identified 707 cases between 1997 and 2009 in which courts made explicit findings of prosecutorial misconduct, 159 of which were deemed harmful.

"As these studies indicate, infrequent punishment of prosecutors cannot be blamed on a paucity of discoverable violations. Even when judicial findings of misconduct result in conviction reversals, disciplinary sanctions are almost never imposed against the offending prosecutor."

## And then there is this...

Stories of prosecutorial misconduct appear in news reports almost weekly.

On December 3, 2011, Jim Morehard published an open letter in the Wall Street Journal (page A15) titled: ***Are Prosecutors Above the Law?*** Morehard was chief of staff for the Senate Appropriations Committee from 2003-2005. He was also a personal friend of former Alaska Senator Ted Stevens and one of four survivors of the plane crash that killed Ted Stevens.

"After federal district court Judge Emmet Sullivan dismissed the conviction of former Alaska Sen. Ted Stevens on charges of failing to properly report gifts, he ordered an investigation of the prosecutors. Quoting from the report, the judge recently explained that the investigators found ample evidence that the prosecution of Stevens (who was killed in a plane crash last year) was "permeated by the systematic concealment of significant exculpatory evidence which would have independently corroborated his defense and his and his testimony, and seriously damaged the testimony and credibility of the government's key witness." ...

"Well, those of us that were in the courtroom during the trial watched Judge Sullivan continually direct the prosecution to reveal exculpatory evidence to the defense after they had been caught repeatedly not doing so. Most of it became public only after the trial. ... The [exculpatory] evidence was persuasive enough for the U.S. attorney general to recommend throwing out the convictions. It most likely would have exonerated Stevens during the trial.

"The first duty of a prosecutor, as an officer of the court, is to uphold the rule of law. By withholding exculpatory evidence, these prosecutors failed to do so. A judge should not have to give a prosecutor an order to follow the law.

"Perhaps it will be argued that charging these prosecutors with criminal contempt of court could have a chilling effect on future federal prosecutors. A reasonable person might respond that charging them might have a chilling effect only on future prosecutors who think they are above the law.

"The Stevens prosecutors—by what the report called 'significant, widespread and at times intentional misconduct'—intentionally destroyed the career of an iconic man who had flown the China-Burma "hump" during World War II and served forty years in the U.S. Senate. Failure to punish them will set a terrible precedent."

Subsequent to the release of the trial judge's special investigator's 514-page report in March, 2012, the Wall Street Journal opined, "Americans hand prosecutors an awesome power—the power to destroy fortunes, and in this case to reallocate national political power. We are seeing a pattern of abuse of this power, in order to win big cases. To help prosecutors remember that their job is to do justice and not simply to defeat the defense team, there should be automatic and severe penalties for *Brady* violations."

*****

In December, 2000, Raymond Bonner, a lawyer, former New York Times reporter and author of "Anatomy of Injustice: A Murder Case Gone Wrong" actively followed a murder case in South Carolina.

Edward Lee Elmore was convicted in 1982 for the sexual assault and murder of an elderly white widow in Greenwood. Elmore is an African-American, mildly retarded with a 61 I.Q. and a sixth grade education. In an Opinion piece, **When Innocence Isn't Enough**, Bonner reports on Elmore's 11,000 day—30 years in prison before being released by South Carolina authorities because of flagrant prosecutorial misconduct.

"Elmore was convicted of this crime three times and each conviction was reversed by appellate courts.

71

Bonner recounted, "On appeal, gone is the presumption of innocence; the presumption is that the defendant had a fair trial. 'Due process does not require that every conceivable step be taken, at whatever cost, to eliminate the possibility of convicting an innocent person,' Justice Byron R. White wrote in the majority in a 1977 case, *Patterson v. New York*."

"The state argued that while the police made some mistakes, none served to deny Mr. Elmore his constitutional rights." "The prosecutor authorized Elmore's arrest after being told that during the autopsy, the doctor found a "Negroid" hair on the victim's abdomen." That evidence disappeared and was not presented to the defense before trial. Some "16 years after the trial, the evidence of the 'hair' was found, concealed in the examiner's file cabinet."

"The retired FBI agent retained by the state to examine the hair said it was not "Negroid", but Caucasian. Mr. Elmore's lawyers had the hair DNA-tested...it was from an unknown man, likely the killer." The Fourth Circuit Court of Appeals found and subsequently ruled there was "persuasive evidence that the agents were downright dishonest," and there was "further evidence of police ineptitude and deceit."

"A man has served 30 years for a crime he did not commit, many of those years under the threat of imminent execution. Surely there are grounds for a Justice Department investigation into whether his civil rights were violated."

# Chapter Six

# Avoid Trouble

*The University of Detroit Jesuit High School is an all-boys school which follows a college preparatory curriculum creating a college-bound culture throughout the school. In my days as a student there, all students attended daily Mass. Religious education set the tone for the discipline demanded by the priests and lay faculty members. Should a student have the misfortune of getting out of line during class hours, an afterschool study session is the penalty. Most students during their four years of the Jesuit education system experience an occasional after-school visitation to JUG.*

*All detention bound students must arrive at a designated classroom immediately after the last class accompanied with their English Prose & Poetry book. On the blackboard is a written assignment for memorization and recitation, a requirement before going home for the day. For example, memorize the first twenty-five lines of the famous Robert W. Service chestnut,* <u>The Cremation of Sam McGee</u>.

> *The Northern lights have seen queer sights*
> *But the queerist they ever did see,*
> *Was the night on the marge of Lake Labarge*
> *I cremated Sam McGee.*

*On the other hand, a student may be asked to memorize and recite back the first half of the Gettysburg Address. "Four score and seven days ago, our forefathers...etc."*

*Bing Crosby attended a small Jesuit high school in Illinois, where he later attributed his ability to memorize so many of his songs to his days he spent in JUG. As a method of student behavior adjustment, JUG signifies Justice Under God.*

---

My mother always told me, "When you see trouble coming your way, turn around and run as fast as you can." In a similar manner, I taught my children, if they should think they would ever need to explain something they did, then just don't do it.

Young people just do not realize that every time they become involved with the law, someone is retaining a record on them. A criminal record is created after being convicted of a crime. A violation of traffic laws, such a speeding or reckless driving, generates a driving record. The National Crime Information Center (NCIC) is a large database of criminal histories provided by local, state and federal police agencies to the Federal Bureau of Investigation (FBI). They assemble and maintain information on arrest warrants, arrests and convictions. The FBI also maintains a fingerprint database named the Integrated Automated Fingerprint Identification System (IAFIS) containing about 50 million sets of fingerprints. There are many other record keeping systems for specific purposes in states and the federal government that keep score on how individuals behave in life.

I first met a neighbor by the name of Roger Smigiel at his home while he was hosting a "meet & great fundraiser" for a candidate running for the county executive. His successful CPA practice allowed him to afford a very large home in a fashionable subdivision. His next-door neighbor, at the time, was the president of the J. L. Hudson Company (now Target). A few Detroit Pistons players lived in homes down the block. They liked their homes because all the rooms have 18-foot ceilings, which better fit their height. Rogers's wife was a lady, just as lovely and gracious as she could be. She introduced their young daughter to all the visitors at the event. They looked like the perfect couple.

Roger provided accounting services for successful professional athletes and medium size corporations. Somewhere along the way, he met a famous retired baseball star through one of his clients. Denny McLain was a funny sort of person with many great stories, somewhat of a raconteur. Roger accepted McLain as a client and began working on his taxes. Roger enjoyed being close to and sometimes involved with individuals living the celebrity life style.

Some months later in 1994, I heard Roger became involved in a big corporate acquisition deal with one of his clients. I am not sure how it all began, but the client was McLain, the retired baseball star. Professional athletes have many statistical records. There are batting records, pitching records and win-loss records, just to name a few. McLain was the last pitcher in the major leagues to win 31 games in one season when he went 31-6 with an ERA of 1.96. He was a winning pitcher and won the World Series and the league's Most Valuable Player that same year. In his ten-year career, he posted a win-loss record of 131-91 and was awarded the American League Cy Young (best pitcher) Award, two years in a row. Now that is the type of record anyone would be proud to have. Roger, on the other hand, may have been better off looking closer at the other records his partner had acquired in his dubious past. The all-star pitcher's NCIC record indicated he had a conviction in 1985 for federal racketeering, extortion and cocaine trafficking charges and received a sentenced to 23 years in prison. McLain's business record was not very good either; he went broke in Florida on two or three startup companies.

This new project, which would later became the problem, was negotiating the purchase of the Peet Packing Company, a company that merchandised various meat products under the brand name of "Farmer Peet." Harley D. Peet founded the Peet Packing Company, the home of Farmer Peet's people pleasing meats. The business was located in Chesaning Michigan on the edge of Saginaw County, 75 miles north of Detroit and 18 miles south of the county seat of Saginaw. Chesaning is a little town in the middle of absolutely nowhere, west of the tiny town of Montrose on state highway M-57, surrounded by farms as far as the eye can see. It is home to about 2500 residents with medium household incomes of about $35,000. The village, where the Shiawassee River snakes its way through the middle of the town, was well known for the

Chesaning Showboat Music Festival and the riverboat named Showboat Queen.

The Peet brothers, Roger and Wally wanted to sell their company, while at the same time protecting all the 160 or so local jobs in Chesaning. The Dorfman family, owners of the Thorn Apple Valley meat company in the Grand Rapids area, had been trying to buy Peet Packing for a long time. A sale to Dorfman would mean a loss of all the Peet Packing jobs for the little town. Dorfman was up front saying he would move the Peet operation across the state and consolidate it into his other plant. Roger prepared a financial statement and presentation while McLain arranged to make the purchase proposal known to the town residents and employees of Peet Packing. McLain had recently become financially well off hosting a morning radio talk show. His radio co-host Eli Zaret once referred to the ball player as a swashbuckling gambler. This business arrangement would even be a bigger gamble.

I ran into McLain at a local charity best-ball golf outing. I came away after the evening dinner with an opinion that he was a world-class bullshitter-con artist. He told me he was on his way to Chesaning to present himself as the savior of the Peet Packing Company. After the presentation, the employees, citizens in attendance and the Peet brothers bought his act hook, line and sinker. The ball player promised to keep the jobs in Chesaning and the company was all his.

The closing on the sale of the business took place within a month and the ownership of Peet Packing Company shifted to the partnership of Roger and McLain. They agreed among themselves that Roger would hold the title of President and the McLain would be the Vice President. Roger took over the responsibilities of overseeing of the company's accounting, financial reporting, internal controls and regulatory compliance. The company continued the contracts with the outside auditing firm and their current lawyers. The first official act of the partners was to set their annual salaries at $250.000 each, an amount equal or greater than the salaries of all the other employees.

The rest of the management team remained in place to continue the manufacturing and distribution of superior meat products. The partners' second official act was to appoint themselves as the pension committee—a committee of two. Anyone should have known it is illegal, under federal law, for a convicted felon to hold the position of a pension trustee. This was the first "Red Flag." Their responsibilities were to oversee the administration, financial reporting and investment activities of the company pension plan. In addition, they had to create an investment policy that performed in compliance with government rules and regulations. As the pension committee, they had unlimited discretion to make fundamental changes in the nature of the investment activities of the pension plan. In short, trustees have a fiduciary responsibility to see that the pension plan is properly run for the benefit of the company employees and plan members.

Soon thereafter, McLain proposed moving the pension investments to one of his friends and financial advisor Jeff Egan, who had his offices in Southfield. The cash flow, in businesses like this, must be accounted closely on a week-to-week basis in order to have sufficient funds to cover operating expenses. Egan, McLain and Roger discussed this move at length and finally came up with a plan to borrow two million dollars in cash and put the assets of the pension plan up as collateral for the loan. The partners were now flush with money. They purchased new cars, covered their country club expenses and obtained a personal condominium in Puerto Rico with the borrowed funds. Roger began to realize that McLain was not being up-front and honest—he was stealing the company blind. Roger continued placing many of his relatives on the payroll, already fatted by the partners' salaries. Everyone was living the high life as the company's sale and profits began going downhill. In a little over a year, it became clear to anyone who really looked, the company was in serious trouble and facing possible bankruptcy.

Using the investments of the pension as collateral to secure a two million dollar loan is clearly an illegal act in violation of the Federal Pension Act laws.

**Embezzlement** is the white-collar crime of misappropriation of assets or funds of others placed in your trust and used for unintended purposes. **Money Laundering** is the taking of monies or funds by illegal means (sometimes using a front man) and making the monies appear legitimate. **Conspiracy** is the agreement by two or more persons to do or not to do something that is illegal for consideration (usually money).

All the Peet employees lost their jobs when Peet Packing Company ceased production in 1996 and filed for bankruptcy. It did not take long for the U.S. Attorney to look into the funding transactions involved at Peet. The loan became due and payable and the banks foreclosed on the assets of the pension fund to recover the unpaid portion. The government charged Roger, Egan and McLain with Embezzlement, Money Laundering, Mail Fraud and Conspiracy. Each of them also became personally responsible and liable for any lost pension funds, by virtue of their fiduciary responsibility to the company.

The U.S. Attorney for the Eastern District of Michigan is the chief law enforcement officer for the Federal Government in the region. We grew up living down the street from one another. He was my brother's age, but all the kids on the block hung out together and played either basketball or stickball in the street. As kids, we called him Joe and still today, he is Joe to us. Joe never joked around about business. He led a task force against organized crime and took down some of the local leaders of the Mafia. Nothing about this case was unusual. While it was not what you would call organized crime, it was white-collar enough to enforce the Federal laws.

The first break in the case came when Egan agreed to talk to the authorities and give them the background to the illegal transaction. He told the Feds he was new in the corporate investment business. In fact, this was the first big corporate client to come into his office and he did not want to miss this opportunity to build his practice. He mostly handled the investments of individuals and had no experience with pension committees and all the compliance laws that made up that end of the business. He had previously handled a few investments with McLain and said his eyes just seemed to glaze over when they came into his office with an account valued at more than $25 million. He described McLain as a smooth talker and detailed how McLain outlined the loan-to-pension fund transaction so clearly. The proposal seemed to fit within all the rules that apply to individuals, rules with which Egan was familiar. Right behind McLain sat the president of the corporation who was a CPA, agreeing with everything the ball player said. Egan said he thought the business deal was legal and acceptable. However, he knew now he was in hot water and needed to do everything he could to extricate himself from the situation. The Feds agreed to reduce Egan's charge to a one-year misdemeanor, if he agreed to testify in the trial against the two pension trustees. They both faced up to 20 years in prison and fines of $500,000, on the money laundering charge alone. Now that is what I would call playing hardball.

The trial of the partners was about to begin. It was now up to the sweet talking ball player to spin his story of justification that a jury would believe. In a few press interviews, McLain denied any wrongdoing and held himself apart from Roger and Egan, claiming not to be familiar with what went on. Roger was perplexed at the time of trial and said nothing. In his mind, McLain was the one who devised the pension swindle and his financial adviser handled all the paperwork. He now realized his partner and former client had turned against him and dissociated himself from anything that happened at Peet Packing, effectively throwing Roger under the proverbial bus. Each had the best attorneys in the Federal system that money could buy, Christopher Andreoff for the ball player and Thomas Cranmer for Roger. As promised, Egan took the witness stand and calmly explained to the jury how the Peet partners contrived their plan to scam the pension fund, obtaining monies financed by the pension investments. Egan admitted making a big mistake for which he would go to prison.

The trial lasted a little more than a week before the jury rendered a unanimous verdict. Both Roger and McLain were convicted of all the charges against them. Egan served his twelve-month sentence in a Minnesota prison. McLain lost his convincing touch and received eight years in a federal prison. Roger received a longer prison term, probably because he was a CPA and should have known better. His wonderful wife, who faithfully stood by him throughout the trial and while he was in prison, finally moved away from Michigan to a small town in Florida, where she obtained a divorce from Roger and remarried. After Roger's release from prison, he too moved to Florida to be close to his daughter. His health was terrible and his former wife and her new husband now became his caregivers. Roger had contracted cancer while in prison and soon died, after only a short time of freedom. This concluded the rise and fall of my friend Roger Smigiel.

The ball player received his freedom from prison sooner than Roger. He was just as arrogant the day he got out as the day he went in. He is but one of many characters I met along the way. I am not so sure there is a moral that fits well with this story. Just remember what my mother told me when I was a little boy. It is great advice!

# Chapter Seven

# Youngsters

*We get it on most every night*
*When that moon is big and bright*
*It's a supernatural delight*
*Everybody's dancing in the moonlight*

*Everybody here is out of sight*
*They don't bark and they don't bite*
*They keep things loose, they keep it tight*
*Everybody's dancing in the moonlight*

*Dancing in the moonlight*
*Everybody's feeling warm and bright*
*It's such a fine and natural sight*
*Everybody's dancing in the moonlight*

*We like our fun and we never fight*
*You can't dance and stay uptight*
*It's a supernatural delight*
*Everybody was dancing in the moonlight*

Dancing in the Moonlight, King Harvest, 1972

---

My practice of law began to develop right from the first day. When I was in law school, like many other students, I often thought I would like to work in the field of juvenile law and help those that seemed to be helpless. One day while in the county courthouse for another reason, I stopped into the probate office and placed my name on the court appointment list for juvenile cases.

There was a time in history when children attended school to the sixth or eighth grade and then they went off into the fields and the family farms to help with the family chores. In those days, the law treated everyone the same way, effectively one size fits all. Around the turn of the last century, major cities with larger populations began to recognize the need for specialty courts to deal with children who ran afoul with the law, known as juvenile court—a part of the probate court system. Society does not hold minors to the same level of responsibility for their actions because of their maturity level and fundamentally because they have not yet grown up and developed fully as an adult. The Court's aim is to rehabilitate a wrongful youth in order to correct his or her ways instead of punishing them for their misconduct. The rehabilitation usually consisted in supervision and treatment for the problem. However, depending on the type of behavior and special circumstances, a court has the authority to confine youngsters for their own safety and for the safety of the community.

During my first case assignment in the juvenile court, I realized the proceedings are not ordinarily open to the public, as they are in adult courts. This incident involved a young boy who ran away from home. His behavior is called a status offense, meaning a wrongdoing only a minor can commit. Similar status acts are school truancy, underage buying and consumption of alcohol or smoking. I quickly grasped reality—it is not so much the winning of the case that is important, but trying to resolve the underlying problems that caused the person to leave his home in the first place. Growing up in my home, we often laughed about the time my sister had a bad day and threatened our mother with running away from home for one reason or another. Mother immediately offered to help her pack her suitcase. This gesture of kindness took the wind out her sails and everything settled down in the house. My client's trauma was not a laughing matter. With the help of the court social worker, I was able to identify the problem, construct a solution to the problem and obtain everyone's agreement.

*****

In November of 1989, two youngsters from the bad side of town, one fourteen and one sixteen years of age were out prowling in one of the nicer residential neighborhoods looking for trouble, when they came upon a woman in her forties. Wanda Tarr was a sales person for the Christian Memorial Gardens Cemetery. She stopped at one of her client's homes to deliver a burial ground deed. The youths pulled their car over to get her attention. She was only a few blocks away from her home where she lived with her husband Glenn. Once they caught Wanda's attention, the boys literally snatched her off the street and threw her into their car. Glenn became worried when Wanda failed to return home in a reasonable time, but did not immediately act upon those feelings. Wanda was taken to Hawthorne Park in Pontiac where she was robbed of $15 and shot nine times. This portion of Hawthorne Park is like a sanctuary setting with trees and undergrowth, not a picnic place with swings or jungle-gym bars or benches and tables.

If that cold-blooded act was not bad enough, Bruce "Baby Face" Michaels and Joseph Andrews Passeno returned to the Tarr residence and told Glenn that Wanda was in some sort-of trouble and they would take him to her. Once they got Glenn into their car, they took him to his local bank and forced him to withdraw $500 from his ATM account. From there, they all returned to Hawthorne Park where Wanda lay dead. As Glenn approached his wife's body, the two shot the fifty-three-year-old General Motors worker six times and left him. Within two hours, they had taken the lives of both Tarrs for a meager $515.

A concerned neighbor noticed a slightly open door at the Tarr residence and checked it out. He found no one at home, which was unusual. He became suspicious and contacted the police. The police put on a full court press to find the Tarrs' bodies and then find their killers. The head of the FBI regional office authorized nine agents to work weekends and overtime to help in the search of the killers. Later people would find out the Agent-in-Charge's home was located in the next block from the Tarrs' home. This crime happened too close to his home, which caused him to make every effort to secure the neighborhood.

The community responded with an uproar. "Something needs to be done about these horrendous acts of juvenile crime," the paper read. High school students armed with weapons causing injuries and deaths had never happened here before this time. Prosecutors used the public sentiment to ramp up the legislatures and create tougher new laws for minors. Then Governor Engler was quoted as saying, "Do adult crime; do adult time," meaning juveniles should be charged as adults, tried as adults and sent to adult prisons.

This theme was echoed during the next election where a female judicial candidate ran her campaign on the theme of "Tough love, tough on crime." She easily won the election to a ten-year term as judge of the circuit court.

The Michigan legislature passed new tough laws to reduce the age to fourteen and lower for charging juveniles as adults, in response to the public's outcry. Michaels and Passeno are now serving life in an adult prison after their conviction of First-Degree Murder as adults.

Prosecutors are aggressively enforcing new and harsher laws, sometimes in questionable circumstances. The county prosecutors are the chief law enforcement officers of each county and they enforce all the criminal laws and statutes of the state. During their partisan election campaigns, like all headline-grabbing politicians, they make promises to the electorate to be tough on crime or be the protectorate of the community. Through this type of political lobbying, many states have continued adopting new laws that allow trying children as adults at younger ages

*****

The urban landscape changes after the sun goes down. The less disciplined, the lawless and dangerous folks, with nothing to do, come out in the open to engage in questionable activities. They do more than dance in the moonlight. Often times their business relates to drugs, prostitution and the consumption of alcohol. Watching the behavior of individuals in seedy places is very educational. "When you just don't have as much to lose, strange how the night moves" Bob Segar once noted.

Sitting alone on a tiny wooded hill in just such a location, an eleven-year-old child watched the activity of a beer store situated 300 feet, or so, away. His build was slight, about five feet tall, sixty-five pounds. He had below average intelligence. Moreover, some would say his mental capacity was that of a six year old. He fired several shots into the air with an old, borrowed, broken-stock .22-caliber rifle. A single random bullet hit an eighteen-year-old customer in the head as he was coming out of the beer store, causing his death. This sad commentary was not going to have a good outcome.

The county prosecutor now had the first opportunity, under the recently changed juvenile law, to charge the youngest person in the country's history as an adult with first-degree murder. The theme of rehabilitation for juveniles had now evolved into one of punishment. The un-chaperoned African-American minor was red meat for the prosecutor to boost his reputation.

The authorities charged 11-year-old Nathaniel as an adult when he was arrested taken into custody. Ordinarily, a circuit court judge would hear a serious crime like this, but the legislature recently reorganized the court system to create a family court division within the circuit court, staffed by both circuit and probate judges. A family court judge with juvenile court experience, who I knew well, drew the assignment to hear this case. The trial judge appointed a local attorney to represent Nathaniel. However, to hear the discourse from the lawyers around town, the judge appointed an inadequate attorney to represent this youthful offender. It is my observation that the unqualified or less experienced attorneys do not make waves in the court process, such as demands for a fair trial or conducting unnecessary jury trials that clog up a judges' dockets. As a result, some judges like to appoint this type of an attorney, more often than not. In the same county for example, another attorney who handled only court appointed cases attached a personal license plate to his car that read "PLEADEM." The license plate told the whole story of how that attorney practiced law. But, now back to Nathanial. At first blush, his unique case was not going receive the level of defense to match its notoriety. Two years passed before Nathanial went to trial at age thirteen. All this time he resided in the county juvenile facilities.

A group of local and distinguished black attorneys joined-in to offer their assistance in the trial; centered on their awareness of the ineffective appointed counsel. In the end, a prominent trial attorney, highly visible in the public eye, stepped up and offered Nathaniel a fine defense, *pro bono*, that is free of charge. The jury of twelve, with only one older African-American man in the panel, found the child/adult guilty of second-degree-murder after four days of deliberation. Michigan uses a so-called blended sentencing law in these types of situations, which gives the sentencing judge discretion when sentencing a juvenile as an adult.

The juvenile court judge sentenced Nathaniel as he would a juvenile. Seven years later, on the day before Nathaniel's twenty-first birthday, the same sentencing judge released him from custody. The mother of the victim who was shot by Nathaniel was satisfied justice was served. The trial judge described the juvenile/adult transfer law as fundamentally flawed and in need of change. This case generated considerable interest and started a debate that is still ongoing as to whether states should re-think trying juveniles as adults. Some say putting children in jail with adults creates super predators. Some studies have found that instead of solving the problem, trying juveniles as adults is making things worse. The Task Force on Community Preventive Services, a panel of independent health experts appointed The Center of Disease Control and Prevention, found the juvenile transfer policies have generally resulted in increased arrests for subsequent crimes (Recidivism).

The State of Michigan essentially raised Nathaniel to adulthood inside the state juvenile prison system. When released, the state provided him with an apartment in Detroit near the Wayne State University and paid his tuition to attend a few college classes. Nathaniel would occasionally make his way back into his old neighborhoods on the cheating side of town where he first found trouble more than twelve years earlier. The inner city of Pontiac in which he grew up is still morally insolvent with no better law and order than back when Nathaniel was kicking the can around grade school.

One night, years later, a police task force staked out target areas to watch for illegal activity. An undercover officer noticed an older model Cadillac in a gas station with its trunk lid up. The police suspected illegal activities, as if someone was dealing contraband out of the trunk. As the officer approached the vehicle, the driver threw away to the side of the car a Seagram's purple bag with the yellow tie string containing a large quanity of pharmacological Quaaludes. That driver was now grown-up Nathaniel. The police arrested Nathaniel for possession of illegal controlled substances. His conviction on these charges sent him back into the adult prison system for three to five years, merely two years after his release from juvenile detention.

# Chapter Eight
# Neutral Judges

*Two roads diverged in a yellow wood,*
*And sorry I could not travel both*
*And be one traveler, long I stood*
*And looked down one as far as I could*
*To where it bent in the undergrowth;*

*Then took the other, as just as fair,*
*And having perhaps the better claim,*
*Because it was grassy and wanted wear;*
*Though as for that the passing there*
*Had worn them really about the same,*

*And both that morning equally lay*
*In leaves no step had trodden black.*
*Oh, I kept the first for another day!*
*Yet knowing how way leads on to way,*
*I doubted if I should ever come back.*

*I shall be telling this with a sigh*
*Somewhere ages and ages hence:*
*Two roads diverged in a wood, and I—*
*I took the one less traveled by,*
*And that has made all the difference.*

The Road Not Taken, *Robert Frost, 1916*

---

My Supreme Court experience gave me a keen awareness of the behavior of the judges I practiced before and how judges should conduct themselves in court. Attorneys and litigants alike expect a court of justice to do justice, at a minimum, as well as appear to be just, fair and impartial in all matters that come before them. A judge should recuse himself or herself, that is step aside and let another judge hear the case, when remaining impartial is not possible.

The grounds for disqualification are typically because of personal bias or prejudice, personal knowledge of the disputed facts, previously representing as an attorney the same parties or having a financial interest in the outcome of the matter. Clearly, a judge's pecuniary interest in the outcome of the case should disqualify him or her from any participation in a case.

Justice Anthony Kennedy of the United States Supreme Court stated that due process requires a judge's recusal "when the probability of actual bias on the part of the judge is too high to be constitutionally tolerable" and where there is a "serious, objective risk of actual bias." Most judicial disqualification rules are regulatory rather than matters of constitutional interpretation.

*****

While on vacation in another state in a sleepy little oceanfront town, I read about a trial that was going to take place the next day and that Mike Sexton, the announcer of the World Poker Tour and Mike Sexton, a member of the Poker Hall of Fame, was in town to be the expert witness. The town police arrested five poker players in one of their homes while playing a friendly game of poker. They were hauled away to the jail in a paddy wagon and charged with illegal gambling, pursuant to a 200-year-old state statute. Anyone could be arrested and taken to jail for simply playing monopoly, under these archaic laws. I wanted to see this poker icon in person so I found my way over to the local court and sat in on the trial. Three things became obvious to me as I walked in the front door of the courtroom where I expected to see a fair and impartial trial. First, the police officers that made the arrest of the poker players were employees of the town. Second, the town attorney selected to prosecute the case was an employee of the town. Third and most important, the judge, who one would expect to be fair and unbiased, was also an employee of the town. The judge received his paycheck from the same municipality as everyone else who was involved in the trial.

I also witnessed an embarrassing display of ineptitude on the part of the town attorney with childish facial expressions used in reaction to the simple and concise answers of the witnesses. He wandered around the courtroom in the presentation of his case, as if he was in his personal playroom. The judge calmly overlooked his co-worker's bad behavior with no admonishment.

The defense proved their case to the satisfaction of the judge, who agreed that poker was a game of skill and not a game of chance. Nevertheless, a week later, the judge issued a big hometown written opinion in favor of the folks who hired him. What would your chances be in a similar situation? Slim and none and Slim just left town. A county circuit court judge reversed the town decision and found the gambling statute unconstitutional.

It seemed to me the participation of this town judge was more than conflict of interest. Scenarios like this are endemic in the town court system and it may also be constitutionally flawed. There will always be some close calls in court cases, but everyone must be assured of the fair and reasonable administration of justice by any judge. Local judges need to be more independent and removed from the immediate relationship with the parties that come before them.

*****

A Citizens Insurance Company TV commercial starts out, "Everyday people choose to do the right thing..." This sentence suggests a common norm. From our earliest memory, our parents taught us to "play fair" and "play nicely." That notion took my me back to the days when we all played in the street in front of my friend's house. No matter if we played stickball, kick-the-can or just plain tag, we had rules to follow, even in the slightest pick-up game. We knew, for example, if anyone hit the ball over Mrs. Allison's car down the street, it was a home run. If the ball went too far to the right or too far to the left, and wound up in the bushes, it was a foul ball. We understood how to play the game, and we developed good rules, even if they were not specific. After a while, anyone who failed to follow those unwritten rules was not asked back to play with us. As simple as that sounds, we could have described our rule making process as our common law. It really did not make any difference what the rules were about; we made up our own rules based on how we wanted to play the game and those rules controlled the game.

Our governmental lawmaking process began as early as the twelfth century in England with the creation of the *Magna Charta,* where people agreed upon the law and it became the common law of England. Many years later, representatives of the 13 colonies gathered in Philadelphia and wrote our Constitution and the Bill of Rights. They declared that no one would be deprived of their life, liberty or property without following the due process of the law. They placed an all-important Due Process Clause in the Fifth Amendment of the Constitution. Due Process forces all three branches of government to follow the laws as written and enforce them in the same manner. Later on, the Fourteenth Amendment applied the Constitution to all the states. So today, everyone in this country, whether a citizen or not, is protected by the Due Process Clause. The standard is that the government must provide proper notice and a fair hearing before a neutral judge before anyone loses his life, freedom or personal property. Through court opinions written over the years, certain due process rights have been further developed and expanded to fit the times we live in. For example, everyone has a right to a trial with a jury. No one is required to take the stand and testify against themselves in a criminal case; they always have the right to remain silent. Moreover, if someone is unable to afford representation by an attorney in a criminal case, a public defender attorney will be appointed by the court to represent him. After a trial, one jailed for certain crimes does not have to endure cruel and unusual punishments. The Due Process Clause requires our various governments and police agencies to play by the rules and play fair.

*****

The notion of a "neutral judge' is an interesting thought. One day, when I was a sitting judge, I received a phone call from Court of Appeals Judge Cliff Taylor, who wanted to talk about a prominent attorney from Southfield by the name of Geoffrey Feiger. Taylor told me he was arranging to have a law professor from the Wayne State University file a grievance against Feiger with the State Attorney Grievance Board. He asked me if I had any dirt, so to speak, on Feiger that I could share with him. Both from the Court of Appeals and later from his position as Justice of the Supreme Court, Justice Clifford Taylor did everything he could to take down Geoffrey Feiger, including reversing large monetary judgment awards. In Taylor's mind, Feiger was public enemy number one. I worked my way up from the streets and have the scars to prove it; so there was no way I was getting into the middle of this dogfight. Feiger filed a formal motion before the Supreme Court requesting the court to recuse Justice

Taylor for the reasons I just mentioned. The Supreme Court was not bound then to any rules on how the various justices would or should disqualify themselves from participating in certain cases, sometimes simply because they are supreme. The Justices of the Supreme Court are self-regulating and did not have to disclose any reasons why they choose to recuse themselves or why they refuse to disqualify themselves. Justice Taylor refused to disqualify himself on the grounds of bias or prejudice. By reading the papers' accounts of this argument, the Supreme Court appeared to me to be amateurish, unprofessional and a bit arrogant. The result of Feiger's motion may have been different had he known of that private phone call I received from Justice Taylor.

Back in the era of Prohibition in a town near Cincinnati, Ohio, the town council wrote their own ordinances against the possession of alcohol. Those charged with the violation of that law were required to appear before the town's special court where the mayor acted as the judge or hearing officer. A fellow by the name of Tumey received a ticket for violating this law, went to court and the mayor/judge found him guilty of possession of alcohol. Tumey took exception and appealed his case through the entire court system of Ohio, right up to the United States Supreme Court. The fines from the uncommon court went into a special fund used to pay the mayor for his judicial work. Tumey argued to the Supreme Court that he had a right to a fair, impartial and neutral judge. Justice Taft, interestingly a former governor of Ohio before his appointment to the United States Supreme Court, reversed the conviction. He ruled the town violated Tumey's due process rights when the mayor, sitting as a judge, had a direct, financial interest in finding Tumey's guilt. I thought to myself, this case seemed very similar to the court arrangement in the sleepy little oceanfront town.

*****

A West Virginia circuit court jury found the Massey Coal Company liable for fraudulent misrepresentation, concealment and tortuous interference with existing contractual relations awarding the plaintiffs Caperton $50 million dollars. Don Blankenship was Massey's chairperson and owner. He financially backed Brent Benjamin, a candidate who was running against an incumbent justice for a seat on the Supreme Court of Appeals. He knew his case was to eventually be reviewed by that court. Blankenship spent $3 million on various committees and advertisements affecting Benjamin's election to the Supreme Court of Appeals. Benjamin was finally elected Justice and was well entrenched in the state's highest court before the appeal hearing of the Caperton judgment. The Caperton lawyers made a motion to have Benjamin disqualified from hearing the Massey appeal. They cited his conflict of interest and the appearance of impropriety because of all the money that was spent on his political campaign. Benjamin found no reason to step away from the case and proceeded to take part in the court's 3-2 decision, reversing and dismissing the Caperton judgment against Massey. Caperton had no higher authority in West Virginia from which to seek recourse, so he applied for review to the United States Supreme Court claiming his due process right to a fair hearing was violated. The United States Supreme Court took the case. Ten state justices and former justices from around the country prepared an *amicus* brief to the Supreme Court favoring Justice Benjamin. They said disqualification matters do not rise to the constitutional level of due process and they presumed justices to be fair and impartial by the very nature they are justices. Amusingly enough some of the "*Amici*" were from Michigan. The arrogance seen earlier from the Michigan justices reappeared. Judicial arrogance has no state boundaries.

The majority of the justices of the United States Supreme Court felt just the opposite and followed Justice Taft's earlier lead, holding that the Due Process Clause requires a judge's recusal. "Our decision today addresses an extraordinary situation where the constitution requires recusal"... when "the probability of actual bias is too high to be constitutionally tolerable." This was a clear invitation for individual states to improve their self-imposed rules on disqualification. "States may choose to adopt recusal standards more rigorous than due process requires."

Back in Michigan, the Michigan Supreme Court looked at their disqualification procedure anew. A shift of political winds brought a new member to the court and a new majority. They adopted a better rule that would now allow the full court to participate in all disqualification decisions "where that justice is unable to render an unbiased decision and unable or unwilling to acknowledge that fact."

A *Detroit Free Press* editorial described the new procedure this way.

"The new rule expands the grounds on which any judge can be asked to step aside. Besides obvious instances of bias (cases in which one of the parties is a close relative, in which the judge has a significant financial interest or in which the judge is likely to be called a witness), the revised grounds for disqualification include cases in which a judges conduct has given rise to "the appearance of impropriety" –a subjective standard that dissenting justices argue will inhibit their own right to free speech as well as the voter's right to know where candidates for judicial office stand on the issues of the day." The new rule also requires all reasoning and disqualification decisions to be in writing.

**And then there is this...**

The Federal system of courts were created through Article 3, Section 1 of the Constitution which states that judges of the Supreme Court and the lower courts created by Congress shall hold their offices during good behavior and shall receive a compensation that shall not be diminished during their continuance in office. They serve for life unless they engage in criminal or improper activity. In a similar manner state constitutions create the various state courts. In

Chapter Thirteen, we see that Michigan, through a constitutional convention in 1964, expanded their court system creating a Court of Appeals and a District Court system. The length of terms and procedure of election were set forth in legislative law. (No more justices of the peace or mayors changing hats becoming part-time judges. (see Page 99)

The idea that judges' compensation shall not be diminished prevents the state legislature from punishing judges for their activity in office or their rulings from the bench. Interestingly enough, Michigan created two additional safety measures regarding judicial compensation. First, they formed a Compensation Committee which set judicial salaries every two years during the last week of the calendar year after the general elections. Offices also included within the judicial compensation group are the positions of the Governor and the Secretary of State in order to insure fairness. The governor cannot receive a raise in pay without affecting the compensation of all the judges in the state. As a point of reference, none of the above has received a salary increase for the past fifteen years.

During the latter years in the 1990's, the Michigan legislature floated legislation which would combine all the trial courts, District and Circuit.
Collective opposition sprang from the circuit judges in the counties of Wayne, Oakland and Macomb. The

objective behind this new legislation was efficiency. There were too many judges in one place and not enough in another. A regional or county chief judge would be able to assign judges where they were most needed, thus requiring fewer judges. This system was one similar to the District of Columbia where a chief judge places fifty or so judges in areas with the greatest need of work. A diverse change came out of the legislation. Circuit and Probate judges were ordered to combine their forces to form a Family Court, and all trial judges' salaries were equalized. Today with the economic turn-down, the legislature has targeted certain judgeships to be eliminated upon the death or retirement of the current officeholder.

Judicial independence should not be confused with judicial neutrality. No member of government or the public should be able to place sufficient pressure on judges to come to a decision which they would not normally reach or otherwise interfere so that a judge cannot impartially make up his or her mind. Refer to the county prosecutor high jacking my law clerk in Chapter Thirteen.

# Chapter Nine
# The Gambler

*"Now every gambler knows the secret of surviving,*
*Is knowing what to throw away and knowing what to keep.*
*Cause every hand's a winner and every hand's a loser,*
*And the best you can hope for is to die in your sleep.*

*"You got to know when to hold 'em, know when to fold 'em,*
*Know when to walk away, know when to run.*
*You never count your money when you're sitting at the table,*
*There'll be time enough for counting, when the dealing's done."*

*"The Gambler"* Kenny Rodgers, written by Lorenz Hart and Richard Rodgers

---

Becoming a lawyer is like becoming a tradesman. My nephew learned from his wife's grandfather the electrical trade. While working as an electrician, he attended the union trade school for five years. He went from being an apprentice to being a journeyman, finally ending with the title of Master Electrician. Law school can consume three, four or five years of your life, depending on how you plan your class schedule. You have to take a test, called the Bar Exam, and join a union, after you have completed about ninety hours of classroom studies. In the early years just like the electricians, one was able to work in a law office for a number of years and "read the law". The employing lawyer determined when his apprentice was sufficiently trained and recommended to the court that he be accepted to practice before the Bar and become a member of the State Bar Association, the group or union that certifies and controls and licensing of lawyers in each state. In addition to providing the license to practice the trade, the State Bar Association offers other benefits to its members. Through a variety of sponsor companies, it offers discounts to members for such products as office equipment and supplies, rent-a-cars and insurance coverage for business, malpractice and disability.

One day an offer to purchase disability insurance was received in my office mail from the state bar sponsored insurance agency. Every lawyer, as well as every businessman, should be adequately insured to cover unexpected future events.

Disability insurance is insurance which replaces a portion of your income should a sickness or illness prevent you from working and earning an income at your occupation. There is always fine print in disability insurance policies that is never discussed. Some policies do not pay your inability to work for conditions such as mental illness or alcoholism or an act of war. Most good policies require the applicant to take a physical exam before the policy is issued. I read over the offer from the Paul Goebel Group and thought it was time to purchase some of this protection, just in case something happened to me. This particular policy did not require a physical examination, but I was in very good shape from years of regular exercising and doing the lawn work around my ten acre homestead. I filled out the form and sent in the premium and forgot about it. The premium for the same amount was paid every six months when the invoice came in the mail.

Ten months later, the morning after my mother's 77th birthday party, I woke up with chest pains running up and down my body. They felt exactly how others describe them—like a gorilla sitting on your chest. This pain was not good news. The EMS was summoned to haul me off while still in my pajamas to the closest hospital. The emergency room physicians told me I suffered a heart attack. The doctors took all the necessary precautions and pumped me full of Valium, before being admitted into the main hospital on the third floor with my own private room. The first twenty-four hours after the onset of a heart attack is very critical for patients under thirty-five years of age. The likelihood of a reoccurrence is great, so the patient must be watched closely. By the time I reached my room, it seemed like I had tubes and monitors coming out of every part of my body. Missing the court dates already scheduled caused worries from the outset. Everyone makes exceptions in a situation like this and all of my cases were adjourned when one and all learned of my illness. I found some comfort and satisfaction knowing the disability policy for just this type of an event was purchased. The doctors kept me in the hospital for ten days, before allowing me go home.

At home there was no energy whatsoever in my body; hardly able to lift my legs when trying to walk upstairs to my office. All heart attacks are serious!
A follow-up appointment was set in two weeks; but absolutely, do not do any work, especially in my law office, I was admonished. In the meantime, the Paul Goebel Group insurance office was contacted and asked for the appropriate claim forms. There was apparently a four-week waiting period before any benefits could be sent out. That gave me enough time to fill out the forms, get a copy of the medical records and properly file my proof of claim. At a follow-up doctor's visit, a new EKG was taken which clearly showed the damage caused to my heart. I was ordered off work for three more months.

As the weeks went by, we all wondered what the holdup was in receiving the insurance benefits. I called the insurance office and they said they were waiting to hear from my regular doctor to review the records of my previous annual physical. It took six weeks before finally receiving a letter from the Paul Goebel Group offices denying my claim for benefits based on a preexisting condition of an elevated blood pressure reading the preceding year. Apparently the insurance policy purchased from the Paul Goebel Group allowed the insurance company to cancel the policy within one year for blood pressure disease. I was dumbfounded and more than agitated. My own doctor never mentioned anything to me about blood pressure issue before this. I felt betrayed by the insurance company, as well as the bar association that sponsored them.

No money was coming into the house, so I began sneaking back to my law office and quietly doing some of my law work. At the same time I started looking for one of my lawyer friends; someone to represent me against the insurance company. An appointment was set up with Executive Director Michael Franck of the State Bar Association to see him about the denial of benefits. Maybe he could help out. As a paid up member in good standing in the bar association, they should be able to do something to help out one of their own. The meeting was scheduled for the next Wednesday in the bar offices in the capital city. Upon arrival, Mr. Paul Goebel, himself, was there sitting next to Michael Franck. The meeting lasted less than an hour. Franck said he was in no position to help me. Paul Goebel said there was nothing he could do; the insurance company had the final word. Here was a one-two punch from the people who were supposed to be on my side to service me. The ride home was a haze for the hour and a half. It was incomprehensible how easily they seemed to dump me out of their office with no assistance. After all I was a lawyer, one of them, and they just threw me out the front door.

Most of my lawyer friends practiced insurance defense work. None of them wanted to touch this case. There was no alternative than to prepare my own lawsuit against the Paul Goebel Agency, the State Bar Association and the insurance company. An associate attorney in my office signed the pleadings as the attorney of record and filed the case in the circuit court. This stressful act was not doing my health any good, but it was time to go to war against these thoughtless people. Why hire an attorney, when I knew the complicated legal system. It looked like another heart attack was heading my way.

It was back to work in my law office in a few months, all the while taking all the medicines ordered by my heart doctor—ace inhibitors, beta-blockers and a cholesterol pill in the evening with a baby aspirin. The pretrial date was set for the next month. Officially I was off work for six months. The associate, the attorney of record, went to the court for the first hearing. The respective lawyers were asked to go into the vacant jury room and discuss the case with the idea towards settling it. Clearly the insurance coverage was paid for in full. Was the judge going to let the insurance company sneak out the back door of the policy, just because a claim for benefits was submitted? The associate called back to the office every fifteen minutes to give updates on the negotiations. At some point, I was asked to consider reducing any future benefits from the insurance contract by fifty percent. I agreed to consider altering the contract if they paid all the current benefits. Based on this agreement to compromise, the judge ordered the insurance company to pay the full amount of my claim. By three-thirty that afternoon, a settlement agreement was drawn up and the case was resolved without the need of my going into court. I finally received a check for my full benefits, one year to the week after my illness occurred. A new name for disability insurance is—survivor's insurance.

We begin to realize our human frailties when struck with serious illness. Events surrounding the illness sometimes prolong recovery, such as lack of energy and feelings of melancholy. The rejection by the State Bar Association remained with me for a long time. In a fall issue of the Michigan Bar Journal monthly magazine, pictures of lawyers receiving awards at the State Bar annual meeting filled a good number of pages, along with the articles about this year's speakers. Right there before my very eyes was a picture of Paul Goebel handing Michael Franck a large contribution check to the State Bar Foundation for $20,000 dollars. Just like a light going on in a dark room, I now realized why Franck, as the executive director of the bar association, and Paul Goebel refused to help me with my insurance coverage problem last year. They were in cahoots with each other; partners in their own interests. The State Bar Association, which was formed to help its members, failed in that regard; but every year Paul Goebel was there with a little cash to maintain his position as the sponsored insurance agent. Now, I better understood how the system worked. The revelation reenergized me to get back into the law game and help the underprivileged and underrepresented break down the barriers of the big corporation fat cats that often squeeze the little guy into submission.

The next Monday, I was downtown in a Federal courtroom, the morning of jury selection for a personal injury case. I represented a little grade-school age girl who received burns over thirty percent of her body from a failed steam compressor. The accident took place at her local grade school. The little girl was returning the daily attendance records for three classrooms to the principal's office. She opened the door she thought was the principal's door and somehow unintentionally walked into the first floor boiler room. This door should have been locked and not accessible to the children, but someone left the door open. No one is quite sure how that happened; but as the little student entered, a switch was tripped and a large compressor exploded. My client was rushed to the hospital with her burns. Similar to the State Bar not assisting me, the school officials blamed the little girl for the accident and offered no assistance to her or her family.

During the morning discussions with the judge, the insurance company for the school and boiler company made their best and final offer of $100,000, in hopes of settling the case. I tried to be as pleasant as I could be; but rejected the offer and jury selection began. Three days later after all the witnesses testified and the exhibits were presented, the jury returned to the courtroom with a verdict in favor of my clients of $395,000, plus interest and costs; totaling to a little over $600,000. I was pleased with the results. The family was also pleased, although the money could not revise some of the residual scars on their little girl. The judge asked me to stop by his office before leaving the building. There, the judge inquired of me why I turned down what he thought was a very generous offer, considering the facts and injuries in the case. I took a deep breath and respectfully said to the judge, "Your Honor, my friend's dad was a gambler and honorable book maker. He always said, 'You lose a lot, when you don't bet enough and win.' The insurance company did not put up enough money for me to bet on." The judge was dumbfounded by that response.

There is a bit of gambler in all of us. But as the song says, "You got to know when to hold 'em and know when to fold 'em." Here, I was able to help beat back the big guys and provide some modest compensation to the little guy.

**And then there is this…**
The Michigan State Bar Association today consists of approximately 42,000 lawyers and judges. From within this Association, thirty-two leading lawyers and

judges established The Michigan State Bar Foundation in 1984. This original group is recognized as "The Founding Fellows." Since that time, a distinguished group of 1464 attorneys have been chosen for their professional excellence and community contributions as Fellows of the Foundation.

The Mission of the Bar Foundation is "to provide funding and leadership, to improve access for all to the justice system, including support for civil legal aid to the poor while providing education and conflict resolution."

Some time ago, I was nominated to be a Fellow of the State Bar Foundation and I am now recognized as a Life Fellow. The lists of the Founders are the names of many good friends I have met along the way over the years. This group has contributed more than $1.6 million to assist the Foundation and its charitable works.

The Michigan State Bar Foundation provides leadership and grants for law-related charitable programs in Michigan and it helps the legal profession meet its obligations to the public. In addition to the contributions from the Fellows, the Foundation receives contributions from tributes, memorials and other private donations, such as interest on lawyers trust accounts, state court filing fees and other state funds for civil legal aid to the poor, such as Access to Justice Fund endowment contributions.

The Foundation conducts two major grant programs. The first is the civil legal aid for the poor program. This provides nonprofit civil legal aid services in all eighty-three Michigan counties. It assists domestic violence victims, helps families keep their homes, assist disabled persons to obtain healthcare and protects vulnerable students and seniors from consumer predatory practices. The program finances nearly 50,000 cases annually, in addition to providing educational materials on legal topics affecting low income persons.

The next major grant program is the Administration of Justice. This grant helps to educate citizens about the American justice system; it informs students and the general public about legal rights and responsibilities; it promotes opportunities for conflict resolution and it provides other innovative law related charitable services to improve the administration of justice. The grant conducts projects such as helping young people resolve problems peacefully, developing publications about the Michigan legal history, conducting training to help educators teach about the legal system. It provides videos profiling significant cases, as well as, establishing innovative legal assistance centers to help citizens with civil legal needs. The goal of this grant is to improve efficiency in the delivery of Civil Legal Services to the Poor.

# Chapter Ten
# Youthful Dream

*You were asked earlier in this writing if you ever considered becoming a lawyer. If that thought even slightly breezed through your mind, see how Connie Marie Skinner made her decision and see how well that decision turned out. It certainly was not easy. "If you are not sure where you are going, you are likely to end up some place—and not even know it." Yogi Berra once said. As you will see, Connie Marie wound up at the top of the legal profession. I quote from the Broadway play* Seesaw *(1973):*

*If you start at the top, you're certain to drop*
*You've got to watch your timing, better begin by climbing*
*Up, up, up the ladder*
*If you're going to last, you can't make it fast, man*
*Nobody starts a winner, give me a slow beginner*

*Easy does it my friend, for that's your life insurance*
*Easy does it my friend, conserve your fine endurance*

---

Kevin Kelley is good friend of some of my companions from the old neighborhood—the boys who attended Catholic Central High School of Detroit. This is a story about Kevin's wife, Connie Marie.

Connie Marie Kelley's father was Chuck Skinner, the legendary football and wrestling coach at Hazel Park High School and later at Birmingham Seaholm High School. Known as one of the toughest coaches to ever walk the sidelines of a Michigan high school, he entered the Michigan High School Coaches Hall of Fame in 1984. Coach Skinner was the father of six children. Supporting everyone on a coaches and teacher's salary was not an easy task, so Coach Skinner went into business for himself—a part-time entrepreneur. He owned Dairy Queens, Putt-Putt golf courses and a resort in Northern Michigan. Chuck Skinner left the imprint of strength, commitment and entrepreneurship on his daughter Connie Marie.

Connie's mother was Anna Petroff Skinner. When she was 14 years old she fell in love with Chuck Skinner, pursued him until he gave up, and married him. Mrs. Skinner had two daughters and four sons. Anna Skinner spent her early family years taking her children on excursions to libraries, bookmobiles and parading through book fairs. She confessed that the toughest part of parenting was "keeping the kids in books." Her children became voracious readers by the time they were in the fourth grade. The love of the written word was imprinted on Connie's young soul by her mother and Connie parlayed the love for books into a higher education and professional success.

Connie's father-in-law was the late great Jack Kelley, known to many as Black Jack. He was a landmark in the City of Detroit, a legend and a mountain of a man, who had more charisma in the little finger than most people have in their whole body. When you saw Jack Kelley, you saw the man who was out front leading the

St. Patrick Day's parade up Michigan Avenue every year. Jack Kelley was a carpenter by trade and the secretary/treasurer of the carpenters union. He served as a council member on the Detroit Common Council for twenty years, after which he served as Deputy Director of Building and Safety Engineers for the City of Detroit.

When Connie was 14 years old, just like her mother, she fell in love with an idea. She had an epiphany while standing on the porch of her Royal Oak home. At a time when other young women were talking about styling their hair and coloring their nails, Connie decided she was going to become a lawyer. Not just any lawyer, since there are thousands of lawyer in the State of Michigan; a lawyer to help others. Connie was full of youthful exuberance and free of self-doubt. She was confident on what the future had in store for her. Back then she did not realize that often times college women frequently studied home economics, nursing or secretary skills or perhaps just to find a husband. She did not appreciate that women who attended law school and passed the bar exam frequently became legal secretaries or research assistants. Connie just knew she would turn out to be a good lawyer. She would need every bit of that resolve and determination to fulfill her dream.

Connie Marie graduated from Bishop Foley High School and began attending the University of Michigan.

After four years of intense study, which included waiting tables in Ann Arbor and Peabody's in Birmingham and borrowing student loans, she graduated with a Bachelor of Arts in Philosophy. At age twenty-two, Wayne State University law school accepted her as a law student. She prepared to take the giant step to realize her dream. The Cass Corridor near the law school became her home. She rented a one-room apartment and proceeded to clean out the cobwebs and cockroaches. This would be her home away from home for the next three years; living side by side with the poor and aimless, those who needed haircuts and others that thrive on alcohol. With her meager memory of high school Latin, Connie Marie began learning about *habeas corpus, res ipsa loquitur*, the Rule in Shelly's case and the Rule against Perpetuities.

Connie Marie needed to continue working to cover her expenses, as she did in her undergraduate days. She responded to a bulletin board job notice at the law school and interviewed for a law clerk position at the law firm of Milia & Kern. Bob Milia, my friend and law school classmate, became Connie Marie's new boss, mentor and friend—a friendship that lasted over thirty years. Bob was just like her father, a non-manipulative man, truly interested in Connie's welfare. Finally, after three years of rigorous academic accomplishment and successfully completing the bar exam, Connie became Attorney Connie Marie, J.D.—Juris Doctor. She worked hard for all of this. Having everything handed to you does not build character.

**If you're going to last, you can't make it fast,
Nobody starts a winner; give me a slow beginner;
Seesaw**

Connie Marie spent the next twenty-seven years of her life following her dream. Her strong background in philosophy served her well as the voice of strength for those that had none. Working full-time with the Milia law firm, Connie Marie went directly to managing the files and clients she most recently only assisted with. Having a fair amount of trepidation, she moved forward, overcoming the fear of being responsible for the welfare of others. She set aside the "fear of failure," which is a constant companion of the trial lawyer.

After several years practicing law in the offices of Milia & Kern, Connie Marie moved on to join Brian Smith, whose law practice developed in a new area of employment law and sports management law. She represented my good friend Detroit Red Wing hockey star Ted Lindsey and other players on the team. She was comfortable representing these professional athletes, since she grew up at the knee of her own all-star father Chuck Skinner. Brian Smith enjoyed having Connie Marie as the point person with his professional clients because of her natural winning personality and her sound legal ability to generate enormous good will.

Connie Marie married and raised three children. She arranged for day care in the home and day care outside the home, while practicing law on a fulltime basis. She was able to survive those years by keeping her head high above the waterline. For the best interests of the family, she limited her practice to part-time occasionally.

*Easy does it my friend, conserve your fine endurance*
*Easy does it my friend, for that's your life insurance; Seesaw*


Connie Marie struck out on her own, forming her law firm in the same entrepreneurship spirit learned from her father. She won a large jury verdict on a discrimination case against her client's employer. And then, Connie Marie took on another colossal case which would become the highlight of her remarkable legal ability.

On a dark rainy night, an excessive amount of rainwater accumulated in a freeway underpass somewhere in the Detroit area. Two unsuspecting motorists plunged into the water-clogged passageway causing a minor collision. While the drivers exchanged insurance information, standing helplessly by the side of the road, another unsuspecting motorist plowed into the same water. He lost control of his car striking into the two innocent drivers, critically injuring the man and causing the woman to lose both her legs before she finally died the next day. Who was responsible for this misfortune? Rainfall is an act of God, Connie Marie thought and she was right.

So she rolled her sleeves up and went to work, determined to find a needle in the proverbial haystack. She researched thousands of documents in the State of Michigan archives before finally discovering the truth. Low and behold, she found evidence indicating the freeway contractors buried leftover concrete debris in the pipes during construction of the road, blocking the proper egress of the storm water which was the cause of the water backup. There it was, not an act of God, but an act of man—a careless, negligent, avoidable act that set the stage for human tragedy, heartache, suffering and loss of life and limb. Connie Marie, with eight lawyers stacked up against her, obtained a $2.5 million recovery for her client's losses. This award did not bring back the lost life and limbs, but hopefully it was expensive enough to get the attention of the freeway contractors and keep them from playing Russian roulette with another's life on their next construction project.

*It's not where you start, it's where you finish,*
*Seesaw*

Connie Marie Kelley became one of the finest trial lawyers in the State of Michigan through dedication and hard work. For her reward, the citizens she worked so hard to help elected her Judge of the Circuit Court, 3rd. Judicial Circuit. Congratulations, we need more judges with her drive and experience.

If you ever thought of becoming a lawyer...if that thought even slightly breezed through your mind, think about Judge Connie Marie Kelley and how she accomplished her youthful dream.

**And then there is this...**
Chapter Ten, Youthful Dream is a story about Circuit Judge Connie Kelley of the Third Judicial Circuit in Detroit, Michigan. She dreamed of being a lawyer from her teens. She became a successful lawyer and culminated her career by being elected as Judge of the Circuit Court. Not so fast...

In Michigan, judges stand for election as non-partisan candidates in all cases except the nomination for seats on the Michigan Supreme Court. Last summer (2012) the delegates at the state Democratic convention nominated two persons for two open positions on Michigan Supreme Court bench and Circuit Judge Connie Kelley was one of them.

While her friends, colleges and supporters worked hard for her success, it wasn't to be. Judge Kelley did very well in the statewide vote count, but fell short in her quest for a seat on the Supreme Court.

Judicial elections are difficult on their own. But statewide elections are challenging and demanding. Read Chapter Fifteen to see how Justice Dennis Archer conducted his statewide campaign for election to the Supreme Court.

# Chapter Eleven
# Offensive Judges

*Detroit was once a nice town. People lived, loved and had a great time. Joe Muir's Seafood Restaurant was one of many fine restaurants in Detroit; but now the original location is closed. In its glory days, when observing Catholics refrained from eating meat on Fridays, the line of waiting customers would wrap around the corner on Gratiot Avenue and up the side street because of Muir's no reservations policy. The law partners of a large downtown insurance defense law firm, Bob Peacock and John Rutt loved the restaurant so much they often stayed after lunch to play cards and have a few drinks. They were usually in no condition to return to the office in the afternoon. On the Fridays when they prearranged to meet their wives at Joe Muir's for dinner, the partners had a waiter keep an eye on the waiting line until he saw the ladies show up. The waiter signaled the partners and they exited through the kitchen and walked around the building to find their wives, as if they had just parked their car in the adjoining lot. "Have you been in line long?" they asked. And no one was the wiser.*

---

When practicing law from my small office in Rochester, Michigan, I often found myself in many courts throughout the tri-county, with every variety of judge elected or appointed to their respective benches, all carrying their own personal baggage. It shocked me to find certain judges were disrespectful to police and prosecutors when a complaining witness would fail to appear in court, requiring dismissal of the case. I found a judge that disregarded a defendant's legal rights and due process while taking a guilty plea by not advising the defendant of his right to appeal the case. One time I went to a court in the next county only to find the judge failed to show up for work that day. It was not only that day, but this judge had excessive absenteeism for the better part of two years. The same judge often missed court at the last minute causing hardship on her staff and everyone involved in the cases scheduled that day. She regularly prioritized personal matters over her judicial duties allowing others to suffer. One time she took time off for professional education. She was followed by a news crew from a Detroit TV station. On the Six O'clock news, there she was for the whole viewing audience to see, shopping for personal items during her working hours.

Another judge had a personal affair with a female while hearing her case. He was also romantically involved with an employee in the courthouse at the same time. Traveling from court to court, I learned about a case where a trial judge failed to make a decision for a period of eight months. When the persevering lawyers brought this delay to the judge's attention, he responded he was no longer interested in the case and had forgotten the facts upon which to make a ruling. It was easy to become disenchanted with how certain courts are handled.

*****

As the legend says, "There are a million stories in the Naked City." A large number of hard working people still live and work in the City of Detroit. Many fewer, since the city turned around. These poor souls must endure the suffering caused by urban terrorists in a social and economic wasteland. Such a person living in Detroit was Walter Marihugh. This 24 year old was electrocuted when he climbed a light pole to steal copper wire and fell to his death electrocuted. His mother said he lived the life of a drug addict. He had little value for his own life, let alone anyone else's property. Similar urban terrorists attacked St. Cyprians Orthodox Church in the inner city by removing all the bricks from the church façade. These predators, nothing but bums and drug addicts, put their lives and the lives of others at risk. An organization similar to the Habitat for Humanity built a home for a poor family. However, before that family was able to move in, thieves stole $40,000 worth of plumbing, sinks, toilets and faucets—a perfect example of the total lack of respect for the property of others.

The parishioners of St. Scholastica Catholic Church on the northwest side held a special mass in the memory of Father Livius Paoli, O.S.B., their pastor and my friend who had recently passed away. Bishop Quinn was kind enough to come and officiate in the religious celebration of the pastor's life. After mass Bishop Quinn walked out the side door of the church to find his automobile. There in the parking, lot located across the street from the former campus of Mercy College of Detroit, he found his lifeless car sitting on the ground with all four wheels removed and missing. Some brazen thieves stole them during the memorial service. The car parked behind the Bishop's car was just plain gone. To everyone's surprise, the car was appropriated in full daylight. Multiply these acts of violence by thousands and you can start to see the true picture of the deterioration of a city for the last forty years—a downward trend since the 1967 riots. Detroit is a city in full moral decay with drug addicts, thieves and violent characters that do not care about your life or the lives of your children. The city is full of dangerous confrontations looking for unsuspecting victims. Nolan Finley of the *Detroit Free Press* authored an Opinion column entitled "How the World Sees Detroit," where he tried to put some lipstick on the proverbial pig.

Cameron McWhirter of the *Wall Street Journal* was not as kind. In his book review of <u>Detroit is the Place to Be</u> by Mark Benelli, McWhirter opined: "Detroit haunts the American mind. For much of the 20th century, the industrial powerhouse of the Midwest embodied the nation's economic strength and abiding love of technology. The Motor City drew migrants from the South and immigrants from abroad to work in its factories and the city's population swelled to more than 1.8 million in 1950 to a now about 465,000 in 1910.

"But since the late 1960s, Detroit has become synonymous with economic calamity and urban decay. Today it has only about 700,000 people, an 18% unemployment rate, tens of thousands of abandoned buildings and a government near financial collapse. Racial tension, violent crime, labor-management strife and public corruption hound the once-great city like a pack of wild dogs."

*****

Michael Wells, a long time security guard for the Detroit Police Department Impound Yard, lived and worked in the city, where the value of life and property deteriorates day by day. Michael's workplace was no different from the rest of the city with the devil always lurking at the door. His job was to protect impounded property for the Detroit Police Department, but ultimately preserving it for the true owners who had somehow misplaced it. Michael Wells made arrests of drug addicts, thieves and violent felons during his thirteen-year tenure as the security guard at the Impound Yard. One could say his job was dangerous by anybody's standards, but he showed up every day and admirably performed his duties and responsibilities. Wells took all this abuse and accountability for the meager salary of fifty dollars a night, not much compensation for putting his life on the line day in and day out. A State Police trooper described this neighborhood as an area he would not choose to be in after dark—very dangerous and rife with illegal drug activity.

Edward Browder, a fugitive from justice, was a professional thief. He was a fifty-one year old drug addict and, often times, he was high on crack cocaine. Michael Wells arrested him one day during an unauthorized intrusion at the Impound Yard and turned him over to the Detroit police. They released him that same evening to continue his nightly terror on the streets. Three weeks later, Browder cut his way back into the Impound Yard, creating a gaping hole in a cyclone fence. Wells saw him carrying a duffel bag full of burglar tools. He again tried to arrest Browder who was stripping out a dashboard from a fairly decent Buick LaSabre. Browder's intentions were to avoid an arrest this time. He threw a tire iron at Wells, narrowly missing his head. Browder then reached into his waistband for a shiny item, which turned out later to be a flashlight. Wells responded by firing a non-lethal beanbag shot towards him. Browder ran off and hid among the numerous impounded vehicles parked on the ten-acre lot. Fearing for his safety, Wells followed up with a real warning shot into the ground, hoping the sound of his shotgun would encourage Browder to keep running and leave the area. There he was. Browder was standing fifty yards away, as Wells unleashed another warning shot into the ground. This time the shot ricocheted into the dark and hit Browder, fatally injuring him. The Michigan State Police confirmed

Wells' last shot was the axiomatic shot-in-the-dark, accidentally killing Browder.

The county prosecutor's office charged Michael Wells with First-Degree Murder, a charge reserved exclusively for the most heinous of criminals. He now needed a lawyer to extricate himself from this mess for simply doing his job as a security guard, protecting his life and the property of others. His attorney filed his appearance for the pre-trial hearings. Things did not go well for him in his effort to unwind the legal web that ensnarled Michael Wells. The circuit judge assigned to the case allowed her arrogant personality and ineptness in the law to become the central factor in the outcome of the two-week trial. She exhibited her bias for the defendant security guard just before the trial began by saying, "Put a badge on a security guard and they think they are God," and "security guards beat people, then lie and deny they did it." These statements came from the mouth of a judge who swore to do justice and to be just— remarks that set the tone for the entire trial.

Michael's attorney made a motion to disqualify the judge. She took his motion as a personal affront and reacted angrily towards him, compounding her previous inappropriate behavior. The judge insisted that she could be fair in spite of her biased notions. Apparently in her mind, it was all right to be unfair and express your prejudice towards the occupation of a defendant, while at the same time, being fair, understanding and respective to the individual's rights during his trial. Wells' attorney realized he had two prosecutors in the courtroom throughout the trial—a two-on-one situation with one wearing the black robe. It was similar to being in a basketball game with the home-court advantage where the referee in the black and white striped shirt was playing on the visiting team.

An expert witnesses testified that Wells' warning shot causing Browder's death was the result of a deflection and thus accidental. The prosecutor's medical examiner said just the opposite while testifying under oath. The best defense, the best expert witnesses, the best lawyering or even the defendant's innocence itself was no match for a judge who is bound and determined to tell a jury to convict.

The Supreme Court approves formal Court Rules and Standard Jury Instructions that must be followed in any jury trial. In the Wells case, after closing arguments, the judge began to charge the jury with her own version of jury instructions. This is where the judge strayed off the reservation. The verdict form created by the judge did not conform to the mandatory state jury instructions. It failed to provide a check off box, which would allow the jury to find the defendant Not Guilty of all charges. In effect, the judge's verdict form mandated guilt of the least offense of Manslaughter.

The jury found Michael Wells not guilty of First-Degree Murder or Second-Degree Murder or Possession of a Firearm during the commission of a felony. Yet, since there was no other place on the verdict form to check off Not Guilty of all charges, the jury, as foreseen, checked off guilty of Manslaughter. Some of the jurors later said Wells acted in self-defense and should be not guilty.

The trial judge continued her condescending remarks during the sentence hearing. "If I heard the case without a jury, I would have convicted you of Second-Degree Murder. And, if it weren't for that one juror, and I want to say it was juror number ten, you would have been convicted of Second-Degree Murder."

I still believe in the jury system, even though I cannot get out my mind this judicial tragedy. It took more than a year to have the Wells verdict reviewed by the State Court of Appeals. It took only moments for the Court of Appeals to reverse the trial verdict and remand the case to circuit court for a new trial. The appellate attorney said, "It is important to note that jury instructions and verdict forms are standardized by the Michigan Supreme Court for a reason, and this decision is a warning to all judges to use them. Unfortunately, this circuit judge tried to reinvent the wheel by creating her own instructions and forms and got it wrong. The result has been that my client has spent a year and a half in prison because the jury was never given the opportunity to find him not guilty."

The Supreme Court affirmed the appeals court finally granting Wells a new trial. Unfortunately, the same trial judge refused again to recuse herself when the case returned to her court, even with all her prejudice exposed. One wonders why the oversight of judges is so weak. Sometimes you just cannot find justice in all the right places.

**And then there is this...**
*Wall Street Journal*, Opinion,
Motown's Mental Breakdown, December 4, 2012

"And make no mistake; Detroit is on its deathbed. Its unemployment rate is nearly twice as high as its surrounding metropolitan region. It has the highest crime rate of any major city because its police force has been stripped (in order to) to pay for retirement bills while two-thirds of the streetlights are broken. Its schools are among America's worst. The city has lost a quarter of its population over the last decade and its abandon lots cover more acreage than Paris."

# Chapter Twelve
# Professor Keenan

*The summer after my undergraduate studies, I took flyer and signed up for the Peace Corps. I shipped off to Syracuse University in Syracuse, New York, for training. The Peace Corps is an American volunteer program started by President Kennedy in the early 1960's. Each Peace Corps Volunteer commits to working abroad in an assignment for a period of twenty-four months. Generally, the work is related to international development. The Peace Corps has three goals: providing technical assistance, helping people outside the United States understand the culture of the United States, and helping United States people understand the culture of other countries.*

*I trained in Syracuse for ten weeks. Each day contained five hours of language education for an eventual assignment in Peru. During training I began to recognize my mission would be in community development; interfacing with the poor people in the community (los populis) who were being murdered regularly by the military for poaching and squatting on rural government lands. Peru's leaders believed if they interposed the American Peace Corp members within the migrant camps, the military would refrain from harming the poor. As it dawned on me that my personal safety and welfare were at stake for the first and only time in my life, I felt I would be better off with two years of law school under my belt rather than two years of "si buenos, gratuitous." Within 48 hours, I was on a plane back to Detroit, looking for a law school to attend.*

---

Every law student should experience an instructor like Patrick Keenan. Pat was not an ordinary professor, nor was he the type of professor who would make you question why in the world you entered law school in the first place. Pat was a very special instructor. He had a captivating style. He brought everything in his tool bag to class every day of his thirty years of teaching at the University Of Detroit School of Law. A former student and now Assistant Dean Denise P. Hickey said, "Professor Kennan had a spark in his eye and a love in his heart for the law that was truly inspirational." Pat once described his technique; "Law School is a conservative place, as it should be in many ways. Dry teaching is the rule, but when there is a topic that is stupendously interesting—after all, blood, guts, death, sex and gore are interesting things—we take full advantage of the opportunity."

Pat grew up in the small suburban town of Ferndale, Michigan where he was the oldest child of eleven. When Pat and I were kids, we usually described the location of our neighborhoods by naming a nearby Catholic church or by mentioning the most notable tavern located in the area. For example: St. Mary's of Redford Parish, on the northwest side of town near Dooley's Bar on Grand River. Pat grew up in St. James' Parish where he attended grade school. As a young man studying his way through Catholic Central High School, he had a higher than average scholastic aptitude. He was member in their Gabriel Richard Club, an honors society and graduated from high school at age 16.

I got to know Pat when we met at a campus event at the University of Detroit. I became fascinated by the fact that Pat was a member of the inter-collegiate fencing team. I tried to play football or play the trombone in the high school marching band, but I never heard of anyone that actually was on the fencing team. Pat wound up attending the University of Chicago, School of Law. I hear that all of the University of Chicago's graduate schools are very difficult and require their students to be smart to get in and stay in. That certainly was Pat.

We lost track of each other until the first morning of the Michigan Bar Examination. We were both waiting to be seated at the Big Boy restaurant in East Lansing, Michigan, across the street from the Michigan State University campus, where the testing would begin within the hour. What a great thrill it was to see my friend after a lapse of three years. Pat was also pleased to see me, but could not believe I attended law school, let alone graduated and was there to take the same bar exam. As we began reminiscing about the past, Pat almost fell off his chair when I told him of my new job clerking for the Chief Justice of the Michigan Supreme Court. Pat knew that those types of jobs were usually held for the best and brightest law graduates and he thought, "What the hell was Sheehy doing even interviewing for such a prestigious position?" Pat broke out with one of his larger-than-life patented Irish smiles, as I provided him with a brief update on my last three years. I smiled back at Pat and my pre-examination jitters began to subside.

Pat lived in Chicago, while attending law school and had completed the Illinois bar exam the previous week. He was as cool as a cucumber. He told me this bar exam was just a pit stop before his wife Marge and he would leave for the Université D'Aix-Marseille in France, where he continued his graduate law studies in Comparative Law. Upon returning to Chicago, Pat began his legal career practicing law at the DePaul University Urban Law Clinic, as well as teaching at their law school.

Foster children under the care of the State of Illinois were being housed in intolerable conditions in other states. Professor Keenan and his law students from DePaul University sued the State of Illinois and took that case all the way up to the United States Supreme Court where Pat argued to bring the Illinois children home. The court saw it Pat's way resulting in the return of several hundred juvenile court wards to Illinois. The decision created many necessary changes in the Illinois juvenile placement policies. Later, Pat moved back to Detroit where he became a professor at the University of Detroit School of Law teaching criminal law, trial practice, torts, constitutional law and professional responsibility.

Patrick Keenan was a flamboyant and extremely popular law professor, one who brought to class every day the flair for the dramatic while entertaining and educating. One day for example, he carried an ax into his classroom and smashed it on the desk to begin his lecture on criminal homicide. He was known to dress in assorted costumes to fit the themes of his lectures. Year after year, the man with the girth of Tip O'Neill educated and prepared his students in legal studies in this manner. Pat said about his teaching style, "A good deal of teaching is lack of inhibitions. It is not a show for the sake of a show, it is a show for the sake of maintaining attention and tension and interest and participation."

Unfortunately we are no longer able to continue the laughs and good times with my friend Pat. He is but a wonderful memory now. A few weeks before a huge retirement party was to take place at the Detroit Golf Club near his home, Pat succumbed to his inner devil, congestive heart failure—a disease he struggled with most of his life. Everyone who planned to go to the retirement party decided to go anyway and the party became a celebration of his life—an Irish Wake for the Keenan family, the school's faculty and students, past and present.

Mark C. Gordon, Dean of the law school, took the lead at Pat's celebration and said a few kind words, followed by various faculty members and former students.

**Dean Gordon:**

"For us as faculty members, Pat was a constant presence. He would sit in faculty meetings with his large yellow legal pad taking notes. He spoke and advocated, but he also listened. He knew how to use the advocacy skills with respect, with respect for the views of his colleagues, with respect and understanding for those whose conclusions differed from his own. And when Pat advocated for a particular policy, you knew his position grew out of a loyalty to the school as an institution, its tradition and its students—which was an intense loyalty indeed. And it was that loyalty and connection to the students in particular which stands out as one of Pat's defining characteristics."

**Professor Alan Saltzman:**

"I never forgot Pat's passion for teaching. He taught important things like Constitutional Law, First Amendment, Equal Protection, Torts and Criminal Law, but the name of the course did not matter. He was teaching how to be a good lawyer. Be direct. Be certain. Don't whine."

**Dean Gordon:**

"One of the first questions I ask an alumnus with whom I meet is 'who was your favorite faculty member?' I think it is with no disrespect to the brilliant contributions, skills and dedication of the current faculty, to say that for the students of the last generation, the name most frequently mentioned to me in answer to that question has always been Patrick Keenan."

**Professor Larry Dubin:**

"From my perspective, Pat wore many different hats. He was a colleague, lawyer, professor, advocate, teacher, entertainer, motivational speaker, collaborator, coach, tough love practitioner, supported of the underdog, loyal friend, media personality and crusader for justice, proud family man and a decent honorable human being. The theatrics he brought into the classroom will always be part of his legend. But the costumes he wore and the luster with which he taught, reflected an underlying seriousness of purpose to develop his students into competent lawyers."

**Dean Gordon:**

"Students in his classroom mention his energy, how he managed to entertain while still educating. They mention his ability to take even the most complex material and make it understandable. And his uncanny skill for making even the driest material interesting and fun. He would walk into class with his trademark suspenders. He would challenge his students. He would question; he would cross-examine. He would encourage debate. And you know he was enjoying every minute."

**Eugene H. Boyle, Jr., Class of '88:**

"Pat Keenan was always smiling, but as a student, we quickly grasped the smile meant different things when used with different body language. A soft smile with a soft look in his eye meant that a student was starting to 'get it'. A smile that involved a shake of the head meant it was not going so well. If you got a smile with a headshake while his head was bowed low, it meant there was no hope. Professor Keenan was certainly an effective teacher in the classroom. He was an absolute tsunami of education. You could not sit in his classroom and not learn. It was physically and mentally impossible not to learn something from this man."

**Dean Gordon:**

"But what made Patrick Keenan so special as a teacher did not stop at the classroom door. Pat was each student's teacher in the lecture hall, but he was also their advocate and their friend outside the classroom. As one alum recently said about Pat in an email: 'He was there to buoy us when we faced adversity and even to smack us with reality when we needed it. You never had to guess where he stood on an issue. He truly shared in our joys and successes—in law school, on the bar exam and when we finally landed that first real 'lawyer' job.'"

**Pat Shelby, Class of '06:**

"To me, the ax, the death mask and the wig represented his passion for teaching. But it was more than acting—he had a tremendous gift for language and vocabulary and such a gift for telling a story."

**Dean Gordon:**

"There are hundreds, if not thousands, of attorneys, former students who are contributing to Pat Keenan's legacy every day. They are the students that made it through law school, at least in part, because of the confidence that Pat Keenan instilled within them. They were the students who were inspired by Pat's dedication and commitment, who learned from him how the law can be used as an engine of justice, who realized under Pat's guidance, through the sheer force of his personal example, that justice is not justice if it is not tempered with mercy and love. They are the students that benefited from his believing in them and who now believe in others. And they are now representing clients, arguing cases and bringing actions on behalf of those in need."

**Ven Johnson, Class of '86:**

"One of the things I do differently because of Pat Keenan is spending time teaching my clients about the system. I talk about the inequities, but I talk about the system being the best system there is. The Professor said to me, "I believe in the system and you should too, even if it does not work out."

**Dean Gordon:**

"Pat, on behalf of thousands of grateful and admiring law students; on behalf of your life-long friends and colleagues in the faculty, staff and administration; on behalf of a grateful School of Law which you always challenged to do better and which owes you so much—Pat, we miss you, we thank you and we love you."

\* \* \* \* \*

Pat was not present for this celebration to hear all the kind words spoken of him, but I am glad you were able to share them with me. You can Google the name of Patrick Keenan and find many, but you will never find another one like the Professor Patrick Keenan I just talked about. All who knew him truly miss him.

# Chapter Thirteen
# Doctor Death

*A long three years of legal studies came to a conclusion. I was motivated by one of Woody Allen's great lines, adapted for this situation. "Ninety percent of successfully completing law school is just showing up." After the final exams, the seniors started studying for the State Bar Exam. This is the only test that really counts because no one can practice law in the state without producing a satisfactory passing score. In those days the bar exam was given at a central location late in July. The results were usually released and made public the day before Thanksgiving Day in November. There is something symbolic about that timing.*

*No matter what the score is of those who successfully pass the bar exam, they all receive the same license to practice law. There is an old joke. "What do you call the person that finishes drop dead last in his law school class?" The answer... "Your Honor."*

---

I was offered the position of Municipal Attorney for the small Township of Pontiac, Michigan, now the City of Auburn Hills, after handling their court business for a couple of months. The position was a part-time client that fit nicely into my private practice of law. I practiced as a sole practitioner from a small two-room office in a professional office building. The practice consisted of general civil and criminal law, preparing contracts, wills, as well as handling divorces, real estate closings, drunken driving cases and small uncomplicated criminal matters. With this new responsibility, municipal law became a big part of my practice. Additionally, this new specialty of municipal law introduced me to new groups of lawyers. I prosecuted misdemeanor cases in the District Court and handled all the civil cases and appellate matters for the township. I advised the council members on law and procedure while attending all of the evening public meetings.

*****

Michigan formed a Constitutional Convention in 1964, to reorganize and update the structure of their state government. The state court system was one of the areas restructured. Hundreds of communities had their own courts for hearing local cases throughout the state. These local courts and justices of the peace did not follow any standard rules of procedure while conducting their business. The Con-Con, as it was called, established the statewide District Court system, along with a three division Court of Appeals. Population determined the size of the District Court jurisdictional boundaries, while the Circuit Court boundaries remained set along county lines. In the beginning, one judge was allocated for each forty thousand people in a district. After a few years for development, the District Court system began hearing cases on the first of January of 1969. All courts now were required to follow the same rules of procedure, rules of evidence and the law, similar to the county circuit courts. All trial judges in the state became state employees, removing any hint of local conflict of interest that is often seen in local courts.

The Township of Pontiac, along with eight other municipal and police jurisdictions consolidated their local courts into a single-judge District Court—no more justices of the peace or mayors changing hats and becoming part-time judges. During my years as municipal attorney, the first elected District Judge was an affable and laughable former local attorney who really had trouble conducting the court business in the new formal manner. It was no different for him than the old justice of the peace system. He was a backwoods type of guy with a tendency to be a little off-center. The week before this jocular jurist took the bench for the first time, he delivered three boxes of pornographic books and material to a younger single lawyer in town. Six years after establishing the new court, this same judge was still goofing his was through hearing cases. He often exposed his prejudices with African-American slurs, just to keep the air of humor high in the courtroom or so he thought. He was an embarrassment until one day, when the word spread; the District Judge had suffered a heart attack and was rushed over to the local hospital emergency room. The next day we all found out, the judge did not make it and had passed away.

The responsibility of filling this vacancy in the district court fell upon the governor of the state. He would use the same appointment procedure to fill vacancies as he had in filing circuit court vacancies. I was called into the supervisor's office and advised the township was going to send my name to the governor's office for consideration of the appointment to fill the vacancy in the court that served the township. The supervisor and the council decided they would be in a better position with one of their own as district judge. The supervisor and two council members made a special trip to the capital city and highly recommended me to the governor, during a private thirty minute meeting. Ten other names of attorneys interested in the appointment began to emerge over the next week. The judicial appointment process usually takes a long time, about three or four months, because of the vetting process each candidate must go through. My odds for this position were pretty good, considering my high-quality work in the court as township prosecutor and because of the strong political support I received from the supervisor and council. Six weeks later I received a personal call from the governor. He made some very nice compliments and asked if I would accept the appointment to the vacancy on the district court bench. With a dry mouth, I could hardly speak, but there was no question what my feeling was when I replied, "Thank you Mr. Governor." It took me two weeks to wrap up my law practice, before I was sworn in to take on this new challenge. The sign on my new desk read: Judge of the District Court.

The first day in court for the Honorable James P. Sheehy was something special. All the lawyers that I had rubbed shoulders with over the years in practice and who really cared for me were there in the courtroom to witness my taking the bench for the first time. Everyone had smiles on their faces, especially Judge Jim, who smiled back at his friends with a grin that just would not stop. It became a little love-in in the small courtroom. After about fifteen minutes of everyone making a fuss over the situation, the courtroom calmed down and the assistant prosecutor called the first case—court was now in session. All my friends quietly left the courtroom one by one and I started the efficient administration of justice that would continue for almost twenty years.

Everything was new to me, my court reporter, my bailiff, my office staff down the hall and especially the citizens sitting in the courtroom waiting for Judge Jim to make a decision. One of the strangest feelings a new judge has in his or her first days on the bench is remembering when to speak and knowing what to say. No other business is quite like this. Everything said in the courtroom is first recorded and afterwards typed into a written record. And once a judge says something important, often times one of the lawyers practicing before the court is likely to respond, "I object, your honor. This is the kind of "ying and yang" that goes on all day, every day in a courtroom. Every now and then the morning paper has an article about the next biggest civil or criminal event scheduled in my courtroom that day. Depending on the seriousness of the matter, I could only guess how many of the press, print or photo media, would try to find a seat in the courtroom, along with all of those scheduled to appear.

*****

The news media reported a story about a doctor who was advertising himself as a death counselor. I was busy at home raising two children along with maintaining my successful judicial career and paid little attention to this flap over what was being described as assisted suicide. Jack Kevorkian, a pathologist from Pontiac, Michigan, publicly supported the cause of patients who are terminally ill having the right to take their own lives with the assistance of their own physician. This procedure became commonly referred to as "physician-assisted suicide." In June of 1990, this topic reared its head close to home, when Janet Adkins was found dead in a Volkswagen van in a county owned Groveland Oaks Park near Holly, Michigan. Holly is a village located in the adjoining judicial district. The county prosecutor, Dickey Tomkins found that Dr. Kevorkian was present at the death scene along with his mechanical dribbler machine. The doctor said Ms. Adkins used his home-made device to take her own life.

Tomkins played baseball for Michigan State University and was drafted by the New York Mets. He went to law school and later became the prosecutor in the county. He was a conservative sort of prosecutor; some would say, a little to the right of Glenn Beck. He had no trouble prosecuting anything that moved. In fact, it seemed to him the court system was nothing but a hindrance to his effort to eradicate crime from the streets of the county. Try to fix in your mind an image of a gallows constructed behind Tomkins's office and you may get the picture. Mr. Tomkins charged Jack Kevorkian with the murder of Janet Adkins. The case was sent to the neighboring district court where District Judge Gerald McNally heard the preliminary examination. Judge McNally had a nickname of Gentleman Gerry because he was so liberal. It was said, he would reduce court fines to zero for those convicted and unable to pay their fines. After a while, the local citizenry caught on to his act and many would plead guilty and claim they could not pay the fine. The Judge would then say something like, "Just try not to do that again", and let them off without paying any fine.

Kevorkian's attorney was Geoffrey Feiger, an over confident, well dressed and damn-smart trial lawyer. His father was a feisty union lawyer, a trait Geoffrey inherited and used well when the occasion arose. Geoffrey had a flair for the dramatic because he was the product of an undergraduate degree in Theater from Northwestern University. Combine the theater, feistiness and experience of trial work and you have a gangbuster attorney. The assistant prosecutor presented the Janet Adkins death scenario to Judge McNally. Feiger did not take much time to get the judge to see things his way. Feiger simply said that Dr. Kevorkian assisted Adkins in taking her own life and no laws exist prohibiting this type of behavior. He was correct and it made sense to Judge McNally, so the case was dismissed without a whimper from the prosecutor's office. The next month, the Michigan Board of Medical Examiners revoked Dr. Kevorkian's medical license.

Less than a year later, a call to 911 reported the deaths of Sherry Miller, 43, and Marjorie Wantz, 58, in a state park cabin located in northern Oakland County. The 911 operator asked the caller if the deaths were suicides. The caller said, "Yes, physician-assisted suicide." Dr. Jack Kevorkian was back in business. The death scene was in my judicial district. The preliminary examination was assigned to me and the hearing dates were set. The small courthouse was overwhelmed with press and media from all across the country. The courtroom was wired for a live gavel-to-gavel television feed by Court TV. We set up a pool media room down the hall for the benefit of the press, as they came in and out of the building. There were five super dish trucks in the parking lot, so that live reports could be sent back to the various television stations on demand.

Most judges have as part of their personal staff the position of judicial clerk. This person is usually a law student or recent law graduate who assists the judge in his judicial duties. Depending on the court, most law clerks are selected from the upper end of their class and are well able to research the law and further assist the judge in preparing legal opinions. As you already know, I was a former law clerk and understood the value to a truly loyal and confidential employee. Clerkships are coveted positions that open the doors to opportunities for new lawyers.

Two days preceding the preliminary hearing of the Kevorkian matter, a sheriff's detective and an assistant prosecutor attempted to tamper with the court and the blind-draw process. The Michigan Court Rule 8.112(b) allows a trial court to issue administrative orders governing internal court management. Criminal cases are assigned to a particular judge through a blind draw system.

The officer and assistant prosecutor spirited away from the courthouse my law clerk, a second year law student who had been with my office for less than a year, under the guise of a secret investigation. They questioned the law student in an effort to find any private or off-the-record information that they could use to disqualify me from hearing the Kevorkian case. They also swore the clerk to secrecy, essentially creating a mole in the judge's office. The prosecutor's office always considered me to be liberal like Judge McNally. They did not want this case treated the same way as was the last Kevorkian case. The prosecutor's behavior was completely improper and unethical. I found out about my clerk's transgressions from an anonymous phone call that night and transferred him to the general clerk's office the next day. Two weeks later, my law clerk was fired for improperly disclosing confidential court information. Had I filed a grievance complaint against the prosecutor or any assistants in his office, I would have had to disqualify myself from hearing all criminal matters until the grievance was resolved—a situation the prosecutor would truly relish.

The scheduled court day arrived and the usual Kevorkian support characters appeared in the courtroom. Mr. Tomkins was the one person always quoted in the press, but he never showed his face in a courtroom. It reminded me of the Land of Oz, where the Wizard ruled from behind the screen. His chief assistant appeared on behalf of the State to present the facts surrounding the deaths of Sherry Miller and Marjorie Wantz. Ms. Miller had contracted multiple sclerosis, which was serious, but in no way was her condition considered terminal. Mrs. Wantz suffered from a chronic pelvis condition, which also was non-fatal. Dr. Kevorkian's attorney, Geoffrey Feiger presented the same argument as he did in the previous case, the women activated their own suicide machines, invented and provided by Dr. Kevorkian, taking their own lives which violated no laws.

During the second day of testimony, both attorneys asked to approach the bench. They presented to me a cassette tape and asked that it be marked and received into evidence. I asked them if they wished to publish the tape publicly in the courtroom. They both responded no, but said I could review it if I wished. The tape contained a video of the death scene in the cabin at the state park. A deputy sheriff videotaped the area sometime around midnight. With no electricity in the cabin, the tape appeared eerie, showing various shades of dark shadows with the two corpses lying side by side on cots. I noticed, while viewing the tape on my home VCR, a narrow table located at the foot of the deceased ladies. Ten or more large hypodermic needles lay evenly on top of the table. "What was their purpose?" I said out loud to myself. If Ms. Miller used her own dribbler machine and started it herself and if Ms. Wantz turned on her own carbon monoxide bottle by herself, what was the purpose of the hypodermic needles in this death process?

Dr. Kevorkian's procedure was to excuse all the family and friends from his "operatory" before any of his deaths transpired. A witness described this event as a "quiet and private moment." Only the doctor and his sister, playing the role of the nurse, were present when the deaths took place. Add to that fact the suicide contraptions built out of a few dollars of scrap parts by Dr. Kevorkian were never shown to properly function as advertised. If I was not suspicious before, I had pretty good grounds for suspicion now.

During the last day of testimony, the medical examiner appeared and told his story from the witness stand to support the prosecutor. I asked just one question. "Doctor, when you examined the bodies of these women during your autopsy, did you thoroughly check both bodies for hypodermic needle marks?" The answer to the question was a resounding, "No."

The bottom line was the State did not prepare their case very well, in this instance. The medical examiner did not appear to be the best witness to properly describe how the deaths occurred. And why not take Kevorkian's sister before a grand jury and squeeze the truth out of her? I felt the prosecutor could present better-prepared evidence, where a jury could conclude the good Dr. Death was the direct cause of the deaths of Miller and Wantz.

With a strongly worded Opinion, I bound the Homicide case over to Circuit Court for a trial on its merits. The Supreme Court later ruled Assisted Suicide was at all times a criminal offense under the Common Law of the State of Michigan. It took five years for this case to work its way through the Supreme Court and back to the Circuit Court for a jury trial. All that time

Prosecutor Tomkins was in the media berating the courts, Kevorkian and attorney Geoffrey Feiger. The public began to get tired of his tirades. After a jury trial in Circuit Court, the jury found Kevorkian not guilty of the assisted suicide charges of the two women. As a consequence of his poor performance over the years, Prosecutor Dickey Tomkins was defeated and not returned to office at the next election.

Ever since issuing my Opinion in the case, I contend that Jack Kevorkian was the only person to read it and take it to heart. He knew that I knew the tricky little game he played in the name of assisted suicide. Dr. Death participated in the deaths of more than one hundred thirty additional homicides, but never again was one performed in my judicial district. His core belief of everyone's right to die was stopped in its tracks after a CBS Sixty Minutes television broadcast. He was arrested and convicted and served 8 years in a Michigan prison. He died a natural death at the age of 83. The dribbler machine did not play a role in his end of life.

**And then there is this...**
In this chapter, I share a fictionalized story of my appointment to the District Court bench for the purposes of describing the process of the appointment of judges. To the contrary, I ran and defeated a sitting judge in 1980 in order to be sworn in the next January.

There has long been a debate as to whether it is better to appoint or elect the judiciary. In the State of Michigan, judges are elected in their districts, circuits and statewide offices and vacancies due to retirement or death are filled by gubernatorial appointments. Many other states fill their judicial benches through the appointment system. The hybrid of both methods is known as the Missouri Plan where an appointed judge must latter stand for a retention-election by the voters.

Some questions in this debate are these:

Will elections make judges more or less accountable?

Can voters and elections do a good job at electing judges?

Do elections or appointments better avoid corruption?

Do elected judiciaries better uphold checks and balances?

Do elections improve the quality of judges?

Which system better upholds public trust in the judiciary?

Competitive Elections are, adherents say, the most democratic way to make judges accountable to the public. But competitive elections have many problems, and critics who cite their heavy reliance on special interest money. 22 states use competitive elections to fill state Supreme Court seats, at least some of the time.

Appointment/Retention Systems, also known as "merit selection," rely on bipartisan nominating commissions to put slates of candidates to the governor, who picks from that list. Voters then periodically vote on whether to retain these judges. While this greatly reduces special interest money, critics call these systems undemocratic. 24 states use bipartisan commissions to help choose Supreme Court justices.

Four states have adopted public financing, as a middle ground, to combat special-interest money while still conducting state Supreme Court elections. But public financing has come under attack and was gutted or inadequately funded in two of these states in 2011.

Recently, I discussed this subject with a newly retired Federal Judge, one who was appointed to his position. I related my style of returning to the jury room after the conclusion of a trial to thank the jury for their service. The Federal Judge said he would never do that to avoid any possible appearance impropriety and he thanked his juries in the courtroom on the record before excusing them. I realized then that my style for personal contact with the jury was an extension of always campaigning and constantly running for office.

**And more**...

The prejudicial sitting judge I described to you in this chapter was truthfully an embarrassment. He remained on the bench for twenty-four years.

One day it was brought to my attention that the crude jurist wandered into the clerk's area behind the counter where all of our employees worked. We only had one African-American employee working for the court at that time. Her name was Gail. Apparently in an effort to electrify the group with his distasteful behavior, the judge got the attention of clerk Gail. In his hand he carried a traffic ticket issued to one Delbert Tucker. The judge said in a loud enough voice for many to hear, "Gail does this ticket say Delbert F\*\*ker?" No one laughed. Undoubtedly this was done to embarrass this particular employee in front of her coworkers. I did not know how to handle such a unique situation, upon hearing about this. Here was a grown man acting like a child. My first thought was to see if the employee was okay and she was. Employees should be treated with deference, given a modicum of respect and never belittled in front of their coworkers.

I had some responsibility to report this event, but it was under no circumstances my idea to have a confrontation with an inappropriate peer. The Fifty-Second District Court was made up with eight judges, at the time, holding court in four different locations. As a group, we selected our own Chief Judge by consensus. At this particular time, the Chief Judge was the Honorable Michael Batchik, whose court was located on the other side of the county in the Town of Walled Lake. So I advised Judge Batchik of the situation and what was told to me by my employee. As far as I was concerned, my role in this matter was complete and I closed the book on it.

The book soon reopened itself. Whatever happened between Judge Batchik and our judge ignited a new bond fire. It was not long after that when I was advised that my fellow judge filed a grievance against me with the Michigan Judicial Tenure Commission. The Commission is a board that reviews the behavior of state judges, magistrates, and referees and holds them accountable for their misconduct without jeopardizing or compromising the essential independence of the judiciary. Usually laypersons grieve judges based upon their behavior in or out of court. I had never heard one judge filing a grievance against another judge. This was first.

The Commission impaneled six judges representing each court, district, circuit, probate and appeals from around the state and invited me and the peevish judge to appear before them. The meeting took place in the Lafayette Building in downtown Detroit. It started out as a normal discussion until the complaining judge commented that he tried to always keep an open mind about me. The judge from the appeals court, Michael Kelly, retorted directly to the petulant judge that he never in his life had an open mind about anything. After roughly one hour of discussion back and forth, we were both asked to go home, make up and solve our own problems. I recall walking back down the marble hallway leading to the elevator where the irritable judge said, "No commission member is going to tell me what to do." This type of strangeness went on for the twelve years we were together at the court.

A few years later, this same African-American employee resigned from our court staff. She then followed up with a Civil Rights lawsuit against the county for employment discrimination on the basis of race, color, religion, sex or national origin. Many of the details of her complaint were not brought to my attention. In the middle of her three day jury trial, however, the county officials reached a monetary settlement with the former employee and the court case was dismissed. This was a good learning exercise for all the parties involved.

# Chapter Fourteen

# Everyone's Lincoln

*A gentleman from a Birmingham, Michigan, advertising firm received a traffic citation in December of 1986. Under the court rules, a ticketed driver may submit in writing an explanation to the judge or magistrate for consideration of leniency. This letter of explanation was received in my mail*

> *T'was the night before Christmas*
> *In Rochester's Hill,*
> *Not a creature was stirring*
> *except Officer Bill.*
>
> *The cop car was heading*
> *Towards the stop sign with care,*
> *In hopes that a runner*
> *Soon would be there.*
>
> *In my apartment*
> *The family was here,*
> *With visions of munchies,*
> *Pretzels and beer.*
>
> *Off I did dash*
> *To the nearest Great Scott,*
> *Of my priorities*
> *Driving was not.*
>
> *A perfect driver*
> *In a world of few,*
> *My record's been spotless*
> *Since 1982.*
>
> *From the store I returned*
> *At a safe speed,*
> *With plates for the dinner*
> *Which most people need.*
>
> *I finally reached home*
> *Front door in my sights,*
> *When suddenly arose*
> *Those flashing blue lights.*

*Twice every day
I stop at that sign,
I guess this day
Was not to be mine.*

*I know exceptions
Are made very rarely,
But on this Christmas
My bills are paid rarely.*

*I was at fault
On this day of December,
But if I'm pardoned
I'll always remember.*

*I really do stop
At the sign all the time,
Day after day
I stop on a dime.*

*As for Officer Bill
He was doing his job,
With no rosy cheeks
Or pipe made of cob.*

*I know he's not Santa
There is no such thing,
But if he forgives
What joy it would bring.*

*As for my family
Their day was the tops,
Mine would have been too
Except for the .....*

*Just kidding fellas
On this holiday season,
I'm mad at myself
And you know the reason.*

*Please do not ticket me
Even though it is your right,
Merry Christmas to all
And to all a good night.*

*From: Ken Regaldo
To be continued...*

Often times when events happen so fast in broad daylight that catches your breath, you need a couple of seconds to sort out what really happened. In the nighttime it is even more shocking, you may need to do a double take or wish for an instant replay. One night about nine o'clock, the sky was clear and the streets were dry, Wayne Fontes, the acting head coach of the Detroit Lions professional football team, was driving his company car towards his home. With four to five blocks to go, Fontes, thinking he was in the proper lane to make a left turn, drove his car right off the road and into a ditch. He was unhurt, but the car became stuck in the mud. He was able to exit the car on his own and walk across the street to a Shell gas station where instead of asking the service person for assistance, he called his wife from the outside public pay phone. Fontes' wife arrived within minutes, about the same time the police reached the crash scene. Fontes grabbed the keys to her Mercedes and drove away from the gas station, leaving her behind to handle the paperwork on the earlier accident. Fontes turned sharply onto Adams Road, while at the same time a police lieutenant arrived on the scene. He saw the Mercedes swerving and pulled Fontes over a block from his home and placed him under arrest. It took all the responders a few minutes of talking back and forth to figure out what happened and who was driving which of the two cars.

The Ford Motor Company owned the ditched Lincoln Continental. William Clay Ford, owner of the Detroit Lions, provided nice cars for his executives' use. A tow truck driver hooked up the Lincoln and began towing it to a storage lot in town. The police talked to Mrs. Fontes, while at the same time the lieutenant questioned Wayne further up the road. The lieutenant finally figured out that Wayne was the driver of both the Lincoln and the Mercedes. From Wayne's demeanor and disheveled look, the lieutenant thought he might be high on something. Based upon this suspicion, the tow truck driver was ordered to stop his truck while another deputy searched the Lincoln for possible illegal substances. Wayne was taken into custody and charged with two alcohol violations while driving two different cars within five-blocks. A quantity of cocaine was found in the Lincoln Continental by the deputy sheriff, whose only business it was to search the car on orders of his lieutenant.

Usually a detained and arrested driver will have his motor vehicle impounded while he is taken to jail. At the impoundment lot, an inventory search of an automobile is conducted pursuant to established police procedures. A search warrant is required for taking a blood sample from a driver when the driver refuses an officer's request to submit to a breath test and the police officer has reasonable grounds to believe the driver has committed an alcohol-related crime, such as Operating While Intoxicated.

This arrest of Fontes was a complicated situation and the county prosecutor knew he had a big fish on the hook. How could he get the most good press coverage out of this situation without offending the deep campaign contribution pockets of the head of the Ford Motor Company? Additionally, there was no evidence available to the prosecutor that would show who was actually driving the Lincoln when the crash occurred. But everyone knew Wayne Fontes was the driver of both cars. Wayne was indicted with a felony charge of possession of illegal drugs, in addition to two drunken driving charges.

After prosecutors and detectives earlier tried to go around the blind draw system by a sinister method of disqualification in the Kevorkian case, I asked the information technology department to design a computerized blind draw software program which would automatically and randomly assign cases to a judge. The court's new blind draw program assigned the football coach case to me. The prosecutor's office did not trust any computer outcome of the new blind draw program. It was humorous to see clerks from the prosecutor's office arrive at the courthouse just to watch the computer make its selection.

As acting head coach of the Detroit Lions football team, Wayne Fontes called a press conference every Monday, after a Sunday game at the Pontiac Silverdome. More press than usual attended this press conference to have

Wayne give details of his criminal charges and explain his involvement. Wayne went into damage control mode. He explained to the press his car was owned by the Ford Motor Company and available for use by all the players and staff of the football team. Thus, the "Everyone's Lincoln" defense was declared. He said he had no knowledge of any illegal drugs inside the Lincoln or where it came from. With that short disclaimer, he ended the press conference and left the room.

The day the Fontes case was scheduled for preliminary examination on the felony charge, another high visibility case was also scheduled in my courtroom. Fontes was trying to duck the media and make his case go away. Unfortunately for him, when he showed up at the court that day, twice as many media and press were there to greet him.

The second case was a murder case involving three Troy High School seniors. They were accused of killing a fellow classmate Robert Delgado because he had gay tendencies and was seeing a boyfriend twice his age. One evening the three young men went the condo home of the boyfriend Robert Andre, just to harass and play havoc with the couple. Things got out of hand and the young men killed both Roberts by stabbing them with steak knives found in the condo kitchen. One of the three defendants had to be tracked down as far away as Port Huron, Michigan, sixty miles north of town, where he tried to hide out from the police.

I heard the murder exam before hearing the Fontes matter. This short delay gave Fontes' attorney and the assistant prosecutor a little more time to prepare and discuss their case. The facts in the murder case were rather simple and straightforward and were all but admitted by the defense attorneys. Each of the three defendants tried to point the finger of responsibility towards the others, in order to lessen their involvement and improve their ultimate position. As it turned out, all three were convicted by a circuit court jury and ordered to spend some term of years in the state prison system.

After a short break for a glass or two of water, the bailiff called the case of the *People v. Wayne Fontes*. Fontes was born of Portuguese parents and grew up in Canton, Ohio, where he played high school football. He went on to college football at Michigan State University before playing professionally for a short time. He obtained a master's degree and began his long coaching career. At the moment he was in a court room trying to defend himself from a big mistake in his life.

The assistant prosecutor presented the facts of the driving accident. The lieutenant testified about subsequent search of everyone's Lincoln. He had no evidence connecting Fontes and the cocaine in the car or any recent use. He just assumed Fontes looked like someone high on drugs would look on the night of the arrest. When asked on cross-examination what standards he used to make that determination, the lieutenant said he had none, just a hunch. The Lincoln Continental was hooked on a tow truck and being taken to a storage lot, when the verbal order to search it went out. The car could have been secured at the storage lot with little trouble until the police obtained a search warrant. The assistant prosecutor argued the Inevitability Discovery Rule to the court. This rule allows the admissibility of evidence discovered as a result of an unconstitutional search, if the same evidence would have been discovered later anyway by lawful means. I decided that rule did not apply where the lieutenant had no probable cause to search the car, just a premonition. The assistant prosecutor continued suggesting alternative laws to have the evidence admitted: the Independent Source Doctrine, the Reasonable Mistake Doctrine, the Plain View Doctrine and the Exigent Circumstances Doctrine. I said the purpose of these exclusionary rules is to deter police misconduct and to promote judicial integrity, so that the court does not become a party to the use of illegally seized evidence.

Without the availability of the drug evidence, the felony charge was dismissed, leaving the two drunken driving charges. During the hearing of the earlier murder case, the lawyers in the Fontes case had enough time to reach a plea agreement for Mr. Fontes—plead to one of the charges and the assistant prosecutor will dismiss the second one. I accepted the plea agreement and sentenced Fontes to a one thousand dollar fine and one year probation. Fontes was ordered to attend and complete a level one, alcohol program. During the probation year, Wayne Fontes was listed on the football programs as the "interim head coach." After ten months on probation, the Lions signed Fontes to a new contract as Head Coach. I sent Fontes a congratulatory letter and discharged him from his probation two months early, indicating completion with satisfaction— an early Christmas gift. Some people now refer to the coach as "Cocaine Wayne".

**And then there is this...**
Cameras and courtrooms have long had an uneasy relationship. Is allowing television cameras in courtrooms a good idea? The legal community never tires of debating the question. Photographers went out of control in court in the early 1930s thanks to a highly sensational trial, and it would take four decades for them to regain it. In 1934, nearly 700 reporters and photographers descended on the New Jersey town where Bruno Hauptmann was on trial for kidnapping and murdering the baby of famous aviator Charles A. Lindbergh and author Anne Morrow Lindbergh. The trial judge allowed still photography, but was unprepared for the barrage of flashbulbs and the presence of a newsreel camera that was smuggled

inside the court. Blaming cameras for disrupting trials, the American Bar Association (ABA) led the drive for their removal. Supporters claim that cameras enlighten the public, while opponents counter that cameras corrupt the trial process and yield bad journalism.

In Michigan, the coverage of judicial proceedings is now permitted, but requests for coverage must be made in writing not less than three business days before the proceeding is scheduled to begin. A judge may terminate, suspend or exclude coverage at any time upon a finding, made and articulated on the record, that the rules for coverage have been violated or that the fair administration of justice requires such action. Such decisions are not appealable. Coverage of jurors or the jury selection process is not permitted. The judge has sole discretion to exclude coverage of certain witnesses, including but not limited to, the victims of sex crimes and their families, police informants, undercover agents and relocated witnesses.

Michigan Court Rule 8.115 governs the use of cell phones and other electronic devices in courtrooms. Each court has the authority to develop a policy for the use of electronic equipment outside of courtrooms. In courtrooms, the chief judge has the authority to establish a policy for the use of portable electronic equipment, like cell phones and laptops. No judge may allow people using portable electronic devices to take photographs of jurors or witnesses, and each individual using a portable electronic device to cover a court proceeding must first obtain permission from the judge. Under this rule, individuals may live blog, tweet or cover court proceedings in some other way if the coverage is allowed under the rules of the chief judge and approved.

Not long after the Michigan Supreme Court approved of cameras in the courtroom in 1991, I was assigned the preliminary examination of the People vs. Dr. Jack Kevorkian. Our court administrator's office was overwhelmed by the number of media requesting permission to bring cameras into the courtroom. The courthouse was small and I was afraid the stress on the building and the small courtroom would be too much. We put our heads together and came up with an idea. Next to my courtroom was a large judicial conference room. Everyone agreed to use a common (pool) camera in the courtroom and wire the broadcast feed through the conference room for everyone's use. There were five large satellite-dish trucks in the parking lot, and the broadcast of the entire court hearing was shown live on Court TV, gavel-to-gavel as they say. To alleviate further stress on the building, the court administrator canceled hearings in the other two courtrooms on Friday. The hearing continued Saturday and the next Monday, which was Presidents' Day, a public holiday when the court is usually closed.

From that point on, cameras in the courtroom worked out fairly well. The role of the presiding judge inside the courtroom is to protect the rights of all the participants. In a sense, the judge plays the role of the producer and director of the court hearing. One day, however, I was thrown for a loop by the behavior of the photojournalists in a particular case. It was the case of Jonathan Schmitz.

Jonathan Schmitz, twenty-six, agreed to appear on a secret admirers segment of the Jenny Jones TV show expecting his admirer to be a woman and not his gay neighbor. When Schmitz walked onto the stage of the taping of the TV show, he found Scott Amedure telling the television audience about a fantasy that involved Schmitz, some whipped cream and strawberries and champagne. Schmitz visibly shaken and embarrassed stated that he was heterosexual and nervously laughed off the remarks. Schmitz had a history of mental illness and alcoholism.

Three days after the taping on March 9, 1995, Schmitz received an anonymous, sexually suggestive note on his doorstep and assumed it came from Amedure. Schmitz went out and purchased a 12-gauge shotgun and drove to Amedure's mobile home. He fired two shots at close range into Amedure's chest. A few minutes later Schmitz dialed 911 from the payphone at a gas station located at the corner of Pontiac Road and Opdyke and said, "I just walked into the room and killed him."

Schmitz was arrested without incident and the Auburn Hills police contacted my office to coordinate a time to arraign him on the charge of First-Degree Murder. A 1:30 arraignment time was agreed upon and the prisoner was brought over to court from the jail lockup. The prisoner entered one door of my courtroom as I came through the judge's door. That is when I was shocked by the behavior of the photographic press. In order to get better photographs, the press had dismantled the jury box and removed all the chairs. The court was in disarray. I immediately left the courtroom and ordered the court administrator to excuse all the press from the courtroom and rearrange the chairs in the jury box. The arraignment took place shortly thereafter without any photographic press in the courtroom. Schmitz was later found guilty by a jury of Second-Degree Murder.

# Chapter Fifteen

# A Good Friend

The letter of explanation which I received from Ken Regaldo, written in verse, offered me a special opportunity to issue my Opinion in the same manner.

Regaldo was ticketed
For failure to stop.
It may have been okay,
But he was seen by the cop.

He responded to this Court
An explanation not terse,
It was sent in a letter
And presented in verse.

The letter set forth
A Christmas refrain,
His failure to stop
He tried to explain.

The message in rhyme
Is truly unique
The Court's tender mercy
Is what he did seek.

The Court will consider
A one-year probation.
If he gets no more tickets,
A standing ovation.

If the Court does dismiss,
Not all will be lost.
Mr. R. will be liable
To pay the court's cost.

Even though you admit
You made a mistake,
With a good driving record,
I will give you a break.

In public life, you are bound to meet interesting people wherever you may go. The Michigan Bar Association held its Annual Bar meeting in Grand Rapids on a beautiful, warm, sunny Michigan autumn afternoon. I became more involved in State Bar activities, so I traveled across the state to attend the three-day bar association meeting. This was a great way to stay in contact with the out-state judges and to connect with the leadership of my profession. While there, I was invited to attend a private reception at a large estate home hosted by the Charfoos & Christensen law firm honoring their former law partner, Dennis Archer. Archer was the immediate Past President of the Michigan Bar Association. He was appointed in January as an Associate Justice to the Michigan Supreme Court, filling a vacancy of Justice James L. Ryan, who moved to the Federal Court. I knew about Archer's legal career up to the time of his appointment, but I never had the pleasure of meeting him. A friend introduced us at the reception and we seemed to hit it off immediately. That afternoon we spent quite a bit of time together getting to know each other.

I stuck around the reception and met many of the judges and their friends, who shared more information about Justice Archer's background. His mother and father raised Dennis in a small out-of-the-way Village of Cassopolis. His dad worked as a caretaker for a gentleman's summer home on Diamond Lake. His mother, a high school graduate, was able to trace her heritage back to a John Carroll, one of the signers of the Declaration of Independence.

They must have been wonderful people and very proud of their son's accomplishments. I am sorry I never had a chance to meet them. Dennis learned much from his father from planting and raising a garden to learning how to work with electricity. As a youngster, he would walk to the Parkshire Golf Course, a public golf course and caddy to earn a little pocket money. Later on he set pins in a local bowling alley. At harvest time he would sell red raspberries or green beans grown in his garden behind the house.

The Archer home was full of love from Dennis' parents who saw to it that Dennis received a proper education. He attended a high school in Cassopolis where the entire village population was a little more than fifteen hundred people. He played on the varsity golf team and varsity basketball. He described his education there as being basically rudimentary, for example the chemistry lab was antiquated. On the other hand, he learned terrific values in terms of respect for people, peers and the older folks. After high school, Dennis moved to live with his grandmother in Detroit. He started taking classes at the Wayne State University and Detroit Institute of Technology, before transferring to Western Michigan University, where he received a degree in Special Education and his teacher's certificate in 1965.

He taught learning disabled children in the Detroit Public Schools.

While teaching in the fall semester, he met Trudy DunCombe, also a teacher. They married two years later. She suggested Dennis attend law school at night, while teaching in the school system during the day. Justice Archer graduated from the Detroit College of Law four years later. The influence in his legal career began to develop around the time he began clerking with the law firm of Keith, Conyers, Brown, Waltz & Anderson. Damon Keith, a partner in the firm, later became a Federal District Judge and then an Appeals Judge on the Sixth Circuit Court of Appeals. Otis Smith, a partner and friend, was appointed for a short time to the Michigan Supreme Court, before becoming Vice-President and General Counsel for the General Motors Company.

Dennis involved himself in the political campaigns of Richard Austin, longtime Secretary of State, along with Attorney Robert Millender. The Millender Center office and residential building downtown Detroit was named after him. Dennis then joined the law firm of Gardner & Gragg. Sam Gardner later became a Recorders Court Judge and J. Robert Gragg was a Wayne County Probate Judge. Gragg was notable in Michigan and African-American history. In 1936 as an Olympic Team member selection for the United States, he refused to participate at the Olympic Games in

Berlin, Germany—a defiant act to the dictator Adolph Hitler.

Then Dennis campaigned for Ed Bell, a former Wayne County Circuit Judge, who ran for Mayor of the City of Detroit in 1973. These fine gentlemen were the leaders of the black legal community of Detroit, Michigan. I was raised and schooled in Detroit and knew most of them. They took Dennis Archer under their wings and showed him the road to his successful career. Just as an aside and during my years on the bench, I was asked to fill in for Judge Gragg in the Wayne County Probate Court, the week after he passed away. That was a great honor to sit in his chair and serve in his courtroom.

The Honorable James L. Ryan, the same Judge Ryan that administered the lawyer's oath to me many years ago, worked his way up the judicial chairs from Wayne County Circuit Court to become Associate Justice of the Michigan Supreme Court. In the middle eighties, President Ronald Reagan appointed Justice Ryan to the Sixth Circuit Court of Appeals, an appellate court that covered four states, with the main Court located in Cincinnati, Ohio. Dennis Archer was President of the Michigan State Bar Association at the time and admitted to having no vision or aspiration to fill the Ryan vacancy. He was asked by a friend to allow his name be placed before Governor James Blanchard for consideration for the vacancy on the Michigan Supreme Court. He finally agreed to be considered for the vacancy to the Supreme Court, after talking over his options with his wife and two boys. Dennis, by that time, had developed a lucrative practice of law and knew he would have to take a cut in pay to accept this proposed appointment. Parenthetically, most successful attorneys that eventually become judges always take a reduction in wages to make that move.

While others were given consideration, Dennis Archer was chosen by the governor to fill the vacancy on the Supreme Court. Justice Archer would become the first person of color in twenty years, since the days of Otis Smith, to sit on the Supreme Court. Justice Archer was sworn in as the new Associate Justice January 6, 1986 at 10:00 am in a Lansing ceremony and, again later that day, at 2:00 pm in a ceremony in Detroit. The Chief Justice was none other than the former governor of Michigan, G. Mennen Williams. He was fond of Justice Archer and became one of his strongest mentors on the bench. Justice Ryan took his staff and research attorneys with him to the Federal Court, requiring Justice Archer, after arriving at the court, to select his own personal staff. Then he moved slowly into the cases that were waiting for his review. The subject of his first case was a challenge to the constitutionality of a new amendment to the Workman Compensation Act which would to become effective in April.

As a trial attorney for fifteen years, lawyer Archer knew the process of the trial judges. However with the Supreme Court being somewhat of a closed group, Justice Archer needed to learn the Court's process while keeping up with his workload. In addition he had to gear up for a general election in the fall, an election to retain his seat on the bench for the remainder of the unexpired term of the previous justice. Archer never held a public office before, let alone run a statewide political campaign. He did, however, have the benefit of being President of the State Bar and traveling throughout the upper and lower state speaking to most of the 108-affiliate bar associations. This was a great opportunity, Dennis thought, to get out and share with the public what he did and how the Supreme Court worked. For all practical purposes, the rulings of the Supreme Court become the final law for almost everyone who would come before the Court. One and all were fascinated by what Justice Archer did and how the Court worked.

Justice Archer's leadership style was that of a consensus builder. He said, "You approach consensus by listening to other's views and then trying to, through facts or law or persuasion, without brutal argument, to bring another or others to appreciate one's suggested, either analysis, approach, or in this case, how the case should come out."

"Our court is a very collegial court wherein we understand the rationale of the others who were either in the majority or dissenting opinions, and there was no acrimony and nothing harsh in our language, whether majority or dissenting opinion, towards the others that disagree", Justice Archer said.

Justice Archer was the first President of the State Bar Association to become a member of the Supreme Court. The wonderful man that he is, that was not the last "first" he was to become. The *Michigan Lawyer's Weekley* named him the Most Respected Judge in the state. Archer stepped down from the Supreme Court in 1990, with the idea of running for the Mayor of the City of Detroit. He was elected in 1993 as mayor to replace Coleman A. Young. He was re-elected four years later, with a large majority of the community on his side. After his two terms as mayor, Archer returned to the practice of law with the Dickinson, Wright, Moon, Van Duzen & Freeman law firm, where he became Chairman of the Board and the first black President of the American Bar Association. Many other attributions have come his way over the years, but the best one I cherish is that Dennis Archer is still my good friend.

**And then there is this...**
After the title on a Supreme Court decision, the first thing you will read is the name of the justice who authored the opinion, e.g. Brennen, T. E., Chief Justice. From the first day working in the Office of the Chief

Justice, I associated with some of the best and brightest jurists in the legal profession. It's not like working in rarefied air; but working hand in hand on a daily basis with those who I only knew through reading the case law in the school textbooks.

I mentioned my earlier friendship with Justice Thomas Giles Kavanagh, which became a life-long relationship up to the day I attended his funeral. Another Justice in the same category was Justice John Fitzgerald from Grand Ledge in Eaton County. His father was the Governor of the State of Michigan during the Forties.

Long-time Congressman William Broomfield of Royal Oak invited my wife and me to the White House in Washington. No, the President was not there at the time, but we saw the East Room and the Blue Room. We had a nice long visit back in the Congressman's office and a tour of the Capital Building. Another time in Washington, I was sworn in to practice law before the United States Supreme Court. Senator Robert C. Griffin moved my admission and Chief Justice Warren Burger administered the oath. The whole experience was like being present in a movie. The Senator's son, Richard C. Griffin is now a Judge on the Federal 6th Circuit Court of Appeals. During that same visit to Washington, I ran into Senator Hubert H. Humphrey of Minnesota in the Senate Chambers.

Years later at a gala fundraiser for the law school in Dearborn, Michigan, Justice Antonin Scalia and I spent some personal time together discussing the process of his appointment to the United States Supreme Court. This is more than a name-dropping exercise. These are the people you read about every day that lead the legal world. They are real human beings at the top of their profession and usually very nice and accessible.

# Chapter Sixteen

# The Sledgehammer Murder

As youths, we watched cartoons like <u>Tom & Jerry</u> or <u>The Roadrunner</u> on television or at the Saturday movies. I recall events similar to the character Daffy Duck hammering another such character on the head with a wooden mallet, only resulting with stars wringing around the victim's head.

One morning at the end of a first call at court, I started to leave the courtroom and head to my office across a secured hallway. As I opened the door from the court, I heard loud yelling by a security officer, "Halt...Hey you get back here!" I peeked around the door opening and saw a prisoner escaping, running as fast as he could towards the exit door from another courtroom. Like in the cartoons, I counted the footsteps and stuck my foot out into the hallway just as the prisoner arrived. He tripped and became airborne, crashing into the glass framed exit door of the building. Within seconds the police arrived as I stood over the crumpled run-away's body. He just groaned at the appearance of the man in the robe standing over him.

The next day the headline of the article in the paper read, "Judge Trips up Escapee."

---

In a *Newsweek* article of March 2007, there appeared an article entitled, *"The Barbie Bandits Get Busted."* Cases seem to take on names that reflect their own identity. Maybe it is just a carryover from my youth. About three in the morning, a 911 call came into the police station from Susan Farrell, the wife of Chrysler executive Terry Farrell, stating her husband was dead in their home. As it turns out the killing of Terry Farrell was at the hands of his stepson Robert Baker, a big strapping guy and a U.S. Marine just back home from an assignment as a White House guard in Washington. This case became known as "The Sledgehammer Murder Case."

When the police first arrived on the scene, the stepson was nowhere in sight. The police developed a working theory that the homicide was committed with the use of a 16# sledgehammer wheeled in a golf stroke manner at the head of the deceased husband while he was sleeping. The murder weapon was not found in or around the home.

The police investigating the murder and relying on the facts as they then knew them wanted to look for the weapon; however, they also needed some permission to search other parts of the home. They recognized, if they screwed up at this point and did not follow the law, this whole case might be thrown out of court at some later time.

A search warrant is an order issued by a judge that authorizes police officers to conduct a search of a specific location. A search warrant describes the address, identifies the persons (if known) and any articles to be seized. Such a search warrant is issued upon a sworn written statement of a law enforcement officer seeking the warrant and requesting a magistrate or judge to issue the warrant based on the probability of criminal activity. With a valid search warrant, police may search a dwelling even when the occupant is not present. The police had a right to look around the murder scene which was the deceased's bedroom, but searching other places inside and outside the home without a search warrant could be illegal.

The investigators followed procedure and placed a call to the judge on duty. My phone rang at about 4:30am and I advised them I was available to issue a search warrant. As a coincidence, the murder scene was less than a mile from my home. The police arrived at my front door in minutes of the phone call. I invited the officers into my home and we cleared off the dining room table and went to work. We prepared the first search warrant for the home and its various rooms.

Before we finished with the issuance of the first warrant however, a new phone call came in from the investigators at the scene. The sledgehammer was still a mystery and not found. The police needed to enter the garage and attached pool house. The police knew they needed a new search warrant to look through other buildings on the property and near the house. I authorized a second search warrant for those areas and the searching continued to preserve the chain of custody of the found evidence.

Chain of custody refers to the chronological documentation, showing the seizure, custody, control, transfer, analysis, and disposition of evidence, physical or electronic. Evidence should be handled in a scrupulously careful manner to avoid later allegations of tampering or misconduct that can compromise the case of the prosecution because evidence is used in court to convict persons of crimes.

Someone must always have the physical custody of any piece of evidence. In practice, this means that a police officer or detective will take charge of a piece of evidence, document its collection and hand it over to an evidence clerk for storage in a secure place. These transactions and every succeeding transaction between the collection of the evidence and its appearance in court are documented chronologically in order to withstand legal challenges to the authenticity of the evidence.

The police who remained in the kitchen of the Farrell home questioned Susan Farrell about the events that took place that night. She was still in her nightgown, covered with her husband's blood, looking as if she had caressed the body when she found him dead. The daylight was starting to show itself and still the weapon was missing. In talking to Susan Farrell, the police found that her son Robert was dating a 17-year-old freshman from Oakland University, located about a mile from her home. Two detectives headed quickly over to the student dormitory to see if they could get any information from the girlfriend. She was located, awakened and not too subtlety advised of her Miranda Rights and the fact she could be charged as an accomplice to the murder.

It did not take much time before the co-ed said that she and Robert took a car ride last night over to the East Side. They parked and canoodled near the bank of a river, with which she was not familiar. There was only one river on that side of town and the police were familiar with that area. Divers found the evidence at the bottom of the Clinton River, right where Robert dumped it. Robert carefully wrapped the sledgehammer at the home in plastic before disposal, which preserved the blood from the victim and Robert's fingerprints. The police started tying together all the elements of his crime.

The police reports indicated Susan Farrell divorced Robert's father five years earlier and she then married Terry Farrell two years later, after a short courtship of less than a year. Robert was serving in the Marine Corps and was away from home until two weeks before the homicide. It seems Terry and Susan had a rough and tumble marriage that contained many physical battles. Often times, Susan would confide with her son about these domestic problems, during their weekly phone calls. For that reason, Robert was never able to warm up to his new step-father. Shortly after Robert arrived back home, Susan broke down and asked Robert to talk to Terry or in her own words, "just do something to stop him from hitting me again." The police now had their motive and the foundation for a conspiracy theory.

A motive is the cause (the why) that moves people to act in a certain manner. Motive in itself is seldom an element of any given crime; however, the legal system typically allows proof of motive in order to make plausible the defendant's reasons for committing a crime, particularly when those reasons may be obscure or hard to identify. However, motive is particularly important in prosecutions for homicide. Murder is such a drastic crime that most people recoil from the thought of being able to murder another; proof of motive explains why the accused does such a desperate act.

The paperwork was prepared and the charging information, an indictment document, charged Susan with Open Murder and Conspiracy to cause the Death of Terry Farrell. Robert faced an additional charge relating to the disposal of the murder weapon in the Clinton River. Both could spend life in prison upon conviction.

The widow mother and her son hired separate attorneys in the defense of these criminal charges. Those who were present at the preliminary hearing could clearly observe the son's attorney was more capable in the courtroom than his mother's attorney.

During the hearing, I made a finding that the evidence presented at the examination supported the son's charge of murder. As for his mother, I went on to say I was unable to determine what role she played in the murder scenario and a jury needed to make the final call on her guilt or innocence.

Defendants are frequently together in a single trial. In this instance, the defendants requested the court grant separate trials on the interconnected offenses to avoid prejudice.

Separate jury trial dates were set, but who would go first, Susan or Robert? It became very clear the stepson murdered his stepfather, there seemed to be no hurry there. Susan Farrell was going to trial first because of her admissions that she prompted her son and she had all that blood on her nightgown at the scene of the crime. Her trial began and it was all over in three days. Susan chose to remain silent and she did not take the stand in her own defense, which was her right. The jury deliberated for a full day before returning with a unanimous guilty verdict. Susan Farrell is now serving a life term in prison, with consideration for parole in twenty years.

The court administrator delayed Roberts's case because the original judge had a heart attack and was off the bench on sick leave. In criminal cases, you never know who will wind up trying your case. Take for example

Judge Ito in the O. J. Simpson case. There is no need to go into any specific details, but it is universally agreed Ito should not have been on the bench for the Simpson case because of his inexperience. That is what happened here in Robert's case. Judge Mary Dingle, recently elected because of her popular family name, took the bench the first day of January. Her legal background was limited to insurance defense cases. She had never handled a criminal matter in her life.

New Judge Dingle had trouble impaneling the jury at the start of the trial. The defense attorney changed his tactic and denied Robert knew anything about the murder. He argued Robert was not even in the house the night of the murder and only disposed of the sledgehammer at the request of his mother. Robert took the stand in his own defense and placed all the blame for his stepfather's death square on his mother's back, clearly showing Robert's ruthless *persona*. The jury deliberated for three hours and swallowed Robert's act, hook line and sinker. They found him Not Guilty of the murder charge, but only guilty of the accessory charge of dumping the murder weapon into the river. He completed his prison term after serving four years of a six-year sentence. The detectives, still today, wonder how in the world the jury could conclude Susan acted alone and doing all that damage with the 16# sledgehammer. She was so slight; she could hardly lift the sledgehammer off the floor, let alone swing it like a golf club.

# Chapter Seventeen
# Good Cop/Bad Cop

*Everybody lies; cops lie, lawyers lie, witnesses lie, the victims lie.*
*A trial is a contest of lies and everyone in the courtroom knows this.*
*The judge knows this; even the jury knows this.*
*They come into the building knowing they will be lied to.*
*They take their seats in the box and agree to be lied to.*

<u>The Brass Verdict</u> by Michael Connelly
Little Brown & Co. 2009

---

When most of us think about the police, it brings back the memory of the first time we were pulled over for a moving violation. Usually the policeman treated us fairly. The police departments come in all shapes and sizes and are more complicated than a layman might think. Over the years, policing became more paramilitary in character, with the increased use of uniforms and military ranks. Their ranks range from officer to corporal, sergeant, lieutenant and captain. Then there is the chief and assistant chief.

The Oakland County, Michigan, sheriff's department is larger than most in other counties throughout the State of Michigan. The sheriff is an elected position and historically police and politicians from all over the tri-county eagerly campaign for this coveted position. The sheriff wears a five-point star badge symbolizing the cardinal tenets of the legal profession: justice, integrity, diligence, loyalty and confidentiality. A friend of mine Tom Quisenberry, a constable from Independence Township, was the father of three boys who became deputies in the sheriff's department. His oldest became the undersheriff and his second had the rank of lieutenant, while the same time the youngest brother, Ken, came along and joined the department. It is said that the youngest child in the family is usually spoiled and gets his way most of the time. Ken became a deputy and his older brothers protected his path. Ken received the best assignments and the best overtime. He never needed to worry about keeping his job during his probation period, as did his fellow deputies.

After some time, Ken Quisenberry was assigned as an undercover officer and placed in a drug enforcement team. I had practiced law more than ten years before becoming a judge. I saw both sides of the law enforcement game. I observed that undercover officers time and again took on the traits of those they were trying to catch. And the deeper they went underground, it seemed the harder it became to bring them back as law abiding law enforcement officers. Ken Quisenberry knew he had to make a name for himself in the sheriff's department in order to live up to his brothers' reputations and in the eyes of his father. He set upon a successful businessman for his mark. Mr. Bellyle owned many businesses connected to the liquor industry. He owned a bowling alley, two pool halls and three bars with pool tables in them. Anyone who knows the bar business understands there are opportunities to separate the various business accounts (skimming) for the benefit of the owner. One of my classmates' fathers owned a bar across the street from the Dodge Main assembly plant in Hamtramck during the 1950s. When his dad retired and sold the bar business, he had been able to save an extra one million in cash from skimming over the years. Mr. Bellyle was no different. He now had five establishments contributing towards his retirement cash.

Congress passed the Comprehensive Drug Abuse Prevention and Control Act in 1970, which authorized the government to seize contraband drugs, drug manufacturing and storage equipment and anything used to transport drugs. The law since then has been expanded to allow seizure of automobiles, homes and money, even property remotely connected to illegal activity. Interestingly enough, the individual forfeited must sue the government in civil court to recover his own property by proving the monies or property forfeited were not part of any illegal drug activity. In the world of civil forfeiture, you are guilty first, until you are able to prove your innocence.

A *Las Vegas Review-Journal* Editorial said it this way:

> "Back in 2000, after numerous documented abuses, Congress reformed the nation's asset forfeiture laws in an effort to better protect the innocent. A decade later it appears time to revisit the issue.

> For those unfamiliar with civil forfeiture, it is a powerful law enforcement tool that allows the government to seize an individual's assets—cash, property, virtually anything—even if the owner of the items confiscated is never convicted of a crime. Unlike in criminal cases, where the defendant is considered innocent until the state proves otherwise, the burden of proof in a civil forfeiture proceeding is on the property owner to show that the items seized are not connected to criminal activity.
>
> \*\*\*
>
> Indeed defenders of asset forfeiture argue it is a vital tool to stop criminals from benefitting from their ill-gotten gains. Perhaps, but allowing law enforcement officials to conduct warrantless searches at their leisure would also make it easier for them. Just because the tactic is effective doesn't make it right.
>
> The concept of civil forfeiture—that the government can permanently seize the property of a person who has never been charged with a crime—seems more at home in a tyrannical dictatorship than in a state founded on freedom, liberty and justice."

In a precedent setting case, Tina B. Bennis brought suit against the State of Michigan for the return of the seized 1977 Pontiac she owned jointly with her husband, John Bennis. Her husband had been arrested and convicted of gross indecency in connection with his encounter with a prostitute. The county prosecutor forfeited the automobile used by her husband at the time of arrest. Bennis argued that the forfeiture was a violation of the due process clause of the Fourteenth Amendment, among other laws. The United States Supreme Court cited a long line of cases supporting the proposition that a person may be deprived of property if it has been used during criminal activity, regardless of the owner's knowledge or participation.

Ken Quisenberry was trained in the nuances of the drug forfeiture law and he artfully used it against Mr. Bellyle. Deputy Quisenberry took one his drug friends over to Bellyle's bowling alley and sent him in the establishment to set up Bellyle. When the drug enabler came out of the bowling alley, Quisenberry followed him into the establishment and arrested Bellyle for dealing drugs. Other prepositioned officers immediately raided all of Bellyle's properties and seized millions of dollars of money and property under the drug forfeiture laws.

Bellyle's criminal case was assigned to me and I heard the evidence at the preliminary examination hearing. The police snitch provided the only testimony of the activity inside the bowling alley. No other supporting evidence was provided. The testimony of a paid witness is suspect at best. The state of the law is not yet to the point of making this type of testimony inadmissible. Deputy Quisenberry raised his right hand, took the stand and swore to tell the truth. I dealt with Quisenberry before and knew his methods and did not believe a word he said. Mr. Bellyle had a great attorney who argued a convincing case, but my hands were tied. The sworn testimony set forth the facts of a crime. A jury now needed to hear the testimony and come to the same conclusions about Quisenberry's frame-up of Bellyle—simply that there was no evidence of a crime.

Mr. Bellyle was convicted in a subsequent jury trial based mostly on testimony of a paid informant—a drug addict and two-time convicted drug felon. The county forfeited over $5 million from Bellyle, his family and businesses. Bellyle and his lawyers fought back on the civil forfeiture and appealed the criminal conviction for the next ten years. Ultimately at age 81, Michigan Governor Grandholm commuted Mr. Bellyle's criminal sentence and his family recovered a large portion of the forfeited millions from the authorities through protracted lawsuits.

Ken's string of luck began to disintegrate. He was caught stealing a car from the police impound holding lot, followed by a motor vehicle crash and driving off, leaving the scene while driving under the influence of drugs or alcohol. This conduct went unchallenged. He was not disciplined for this behavior due to his brothers working in the department. Not too long after however, the air came out of Ken's balloon and he retired. His brothers retired and were no longer available to cover up his unethical and immoral comportment.

Throughout my career, I was promised promotions and appointments from the sitting governor. Those did not always pan-out as agreed. See if you can appreciate this.

One person who was eager to run for the elected office of sheriff was a seasoned police veteran named John Nichols. John had been a precinct inspector at the Joy Road/ Petoskey precinct and former chief of police for the City of Detroit. He ran for Oakland County sheriff, after retiring from Detroit, and was elected. He maintained that position for many years past the time one should normally retire. Nichols liked to hire recruits away from the Detroit department, because he knew how well they were trained. One young man he went after was Mike Raleigh, whose parents owned the Raleigh House restaurant, a famous old-line restaurant in the area. Mike, a good looking Irish kid, became a favorite of the sheriff. Mike went through the regular road patrol progression and was called in for special assignments when the sheriff went out to make his personal appearances. Mike was right there next to the sheriff, not so much as a body guard, but to put a younger and polished face on the department.

Nichols treated Mike Raleigh as if he were his son. It was not long before Mike was promoted to the rank of sergeant to become the command officer for the afternoon patrol officers. He took the lead in developing sub-stations in various strategic parts of the county. The City of Rochester Hills chose to subcontract their police protection with the sheriff's department. And as the city grew over the years, so did the size of the number of deputies needed to patrol the city.

Using the sheriff's department for policing services ensured the city to an unlimited number of deputies present in the city, in case of a crisis. One day, for instance, with no warning, the building at the intersection of the two main streets blew up from a gas leak causing a large concussion that could be felt two miles away. Within five minutes the whole town was cordoned off to allow emergency fire and gas company vehicles in to control the situation. The traffic was quickly rerouted around the streets where bricks from the building flew more than fifty yards. After this incident the city father's began to beef up the police protection and added more deputies for better coverage of the city. With this expansion, the city built a new substation/fire hall as close to the center of the city as possible. Sergeant Mike Raleigh was promoted to the rank of Captain and assigned to run the newly named Sheriff John Nichols Substation.

You hear of someone being the youngest to accomplish this or that, but Mike Raleigh was in his middle thirties, pretty young for an important command position like this. He was doing a great job and was always present at the city's public hearings. He constantly arrived with a smile on his face backed up with his good looks and charm. I suspect there was a little jealousy somewhere in the ranks. Rumors were overheard that Mike had been tapped by the sheriff to be his successor when the sheriff chose to step down and retire. Now was the time to give Mike the credentials he would need to make the next step. He was authorized to attend the FBI Police School in Quantico, Virginia to complete the six-month training course. During that period he continued his command of the Nichols substation. He even flew home on the weekends so he could be in the office and complete his paperwork. He accomplished everything that was asked of him without any complaints about his governance.

One time Captain Mike returned to town from training just to show up at an official and social event beside Sheriff Nichols and Mrs. Nichols. Somewhere along the way Mike fell out of grace with the either the sheriff or his wife and the sheriff was persuaded to move Mike to the side. Seems like all the advertising and the talk about Mike succeeding the sheriff pushed Captain Mike Raleigh too far into the limelight making him exceptionally popular; too much apparently for the sheriff and his wife.

The sheriff and the county prosecutor came up with the concept of opening an investigation, something short of a grand jury, in order to dirty the public image of Mike and run the whole process through the prosecutor's office to save the sheriff public embarrassment. The first step was for the sheriff to have a confidential disciplinary hearing. The details could be kept secret from the public as an exception to the Freedom of Information Act. Mike Raleigh was busted to the rank of sergeant, as a result of the hearing. Mistrustful comments began to leak out which gave the prosecutor the ammunition he needed to start his probe.

It was not long before the county prosecutor prepared indictments against Mike Raleigh and four other deputies. Charging additional persons was a way for the prosecutor to claim he was cleaning up all the criminal activity in the sheriff's department and not just getting back at Mike Raleigh. The prosecutor was quoted in the paper as saying these charges "would cut off the head of the snake of all criminal activity in the county." The charges were filed and once again, assistant prosecutors came to the clerk's office in my courthouse to watch the blind draw computer, hoping that I was not assigned the cases in which Raleigh was involved. The charges against the five deputies were dispersed to five different courts with five different judges. I was not assigned the Raleigh case. I was assigned a separate case charging a Deputy Ron Casacelli with the crime of Larceny over $100.

Mike Raleigh was charged with forty-five felonies and one misdemeanor. The felonies were of one nature or another, but intriguingly, the charges were written under the common law. Keep in mind, Michigan is a statutory state and the legislature has written all of the criminal code into law. There was no need for the prosecutor to fabricate the common law because the criminal code already provides a sufficient means for criminal charges. This became a big red flag to anyone who knew anything about criminal procedure. Another judge in our court heard the preliminary examination on the first forty-five felonies over a period of two weeks. His decision for dismissing all charges was based on insufficient evidence to prove the elements of the respective crimes. Six months later a jury was selected to hear the one misdemeanor case. After a week-long trial and deliberation, the jury found Mike not guilty and the judge dismissed that charge. Mike Raleigh was suspended from the sheriff's department without pay for this entire period.

The case assigned to me was out of the ordinary, when you take into account what was considered a major crime on the county level. When Mike Raleigh was on his way up the police ladder and times were better, the deputies from the substation arranged a holiday party and invited Sheriff Nichols as their special guest. The gift committee thought of giving the sheriff and Captain Raleigh similar gifts. Ron Casacelli came up with the idea of presenting them with refurbished police call boxes used many years ago inside the City of Detroit, keeping in mind that both Raleigh and the sheriff started their police careers in Detroit. Ron went to Detroit one night and removed two antiquated police call boxes from the wall of the Southfield freeway. The use of call boxes had been abandoned twenty-five years earlier. In fact, one could find a mountain of old removed call boxes in a large pile at the rear of the impound lot. Casacelli restored and painted the boxes he hand-picked at a local collision shop and rewired them with good phones. He placed little gold plaques on the front and presented them to the sheriff and captain at the Christmas party. Both gentlemen hung them in their office with pride. During the investigation of Captain Raleigh, his office was searched and the call box was removed to be used as evidence.

At Casacelli's preliminary examination hearing, the prosecutor called the Auditor of the City of Detroit to testify to the value of the stolen property. He brought books and records to show the city paid around six hundred dollars to install the boxes when they were brand new. The prosecutor failed to mention (read: concealed the truth or lied) anyone could buy the boxes from the city for three dollars. The third witness to everyone's surprise was Sheriff John Nichols. He took the stand in all his military glory, like McArthur returning from the war. After all the questions were asked, I had to ask a few of my own. I inquired if all his mementos from the sheriff's career on the wall in his office were also stolen at some time or another from the City of Detroit, especially the Petoskey/Joy Road street sign on the corner in front of the precinct station. At that point Sheriff Nichols clammed up and almost took the Fifth Amendment. I saw this case for what it was; a scam by the prosecutor's office created only to give some legitimacy to firing Captain Raleigh.

Mike Raleigh's problems continued for the better part of the next three years. All of the related cases heard before the five individual judges were dismissed by each judge, after full and fair hearings. The courts had spoken—there was no crime in the sheriff's department and all these gentlemen should go back to work, after their suspensions. But no, the prosecutor was not finished. He appealed all of the cases to every level of the state court system, Circuit Court, Court of Appeals and the Supreme Court. All the courts rejected each and every claim of the prosecutor—an exercise in futility. Raleigh sued the county for his unlawful discharge in the Federal District Court. By the time that case made it to trial, the county finally gave in and surrendered. All the deputies were allowed to return to work and given their back wages. Raleigh was reinstated to the rank of Sergeant, given all his back pay and allowed to retired the next day with full retirement benefits. The county grudgingly paid his attorney fees for the past five years. This was a hard and long road for Raleigh to get his good reputation back.

Reading this you must ask yourself who actually was the good cop and who was the bad cop. Well Kenny, the cop who tried to make himself a good name, was categorically a bad cop. And the Raleigh, who the prosecutor tried to show as the bad cop, was the good cop. Mike Raleigh, the good cop, continues to be a really good guy today.

**And then there is this...**
At the end of Chapter One, I related to you my assignment as a senior visiting judge in the City of Pontiac during 2008. Many events took place that year which made the year noteworthy.

During the month of March, along with taking on this judicial position, my brother Mike was diagnosed with having pancreatic cancer. There is not much good one can say about that disease. The only blessing is that I was able to be in the Detroit area and spend his last months together with him.

My father passed in 1952 and my mother purchased six burial plots at White Chapel Memorial Cemetery located in the City of Troy. Both my parents are now buried there, along with the ashes of my brother Dan. It was time to do business with the cemetery office and prepare for the inevitability facing my brother and his family.

On one sunny summer morning, my wife and I drove over to White Chapel in an attempt to acquire the appropriate paperwork to complete in advance. Our wives asked that their names be placed into the office file. The gentleman clerk I dealt with was very cooperative; however, he advised me there would be a $150 fee for that service. I asked him what the fee was about. He advised me that it was a filing fee and was required by the owners of the cemetery. My lawyer instincts came to the forefront and I decided not to deal with this issue until I was able to learn more about the cemetery process.

"Cemeteries are not governed by laws that apply to real property due to their inherently different nature. Most states have established laws that specifically apply to cemeteries.

"The purchaser of a plot in a cemetery is generally regarded as having obtained only a limited property right. He or she acquires a privilege or license to make burials in the purchased plot, exclusive of all other people, provided that the land remains a cemetery."
TheFreeDictionary: Title and Rights of Owners of Grave Plots.

Unfortunately, the inescapable took place as my brother passed during the month of August. The whole family gathered gave "good ole Mike" a very appropriate funeral and proper send off with his gravesite service at White Chapel. After the funeral, I continued with my work at the Pontiac Court as visiting judge.

Shortly after that, I located the name of the attorney who represented the cemetery corporation. I connected by phone after two or three tries. The conversation centered on the need for a filing fee. This attorney tried to explain to me that it was similar to filing a new title on a piece of real estate. I knew that not to be true. I just had a right to be buried there. The young attorney added, "We have rules around here and we have to follow the rules."

Wow! Slam the door on me, why don't you.

From time to time, we hear about relatives of a deceased having dreams or communications with the dearly departed. I am not sure I believe in all of that, but try this on for size. What are the odds my brother Mike may have had anything to do with this?

About three weeks later on September 15th, my courtroom mission was to handle a large collection of traffic citations. Basically, three or four police officers appear in court with the traffic tickets they issued during the previous month. I shuffled through the pile of tickets and put them in order by way of which officer issued them. At that point each police officer exits to the hallway and discusses with the each respective driver how he or she wishes to handle their case.

Believe it or not, I immediately recognized the name of the young attorney who represented the cemetery corporation on Officer Green's list of cases. I set that particular ticket aside because I needed time to think of the ramifications regarding our previous discussion. I decided to handle that matter last, when the courtroom was all but empty.

"Officer Green, how do you wish to proceed with this matter?" I said

"Your Honor, my witnesses have failed to appear this morning. Therefore, I wish to dismiss this ticket." The whole case was back on my shoulders. I had options which I explained to the now nervous lawyer. I could grant the officer's request or adjourn the case until such time as the witnesses could be subpoenaed to appear for trial.

By this time, it was late in the morning. What are the chances that this particular individual found his way onto my docket in a neighboring city? It was like he hit the lottery! Did my brother have any involvement in this situation, keeping in mind he now resided in White Chapel? I re-introduced myself to the cemetery attorney as the Jim Sheehy he recently spoke to on the phone. I talked a little about dealing with people and how I tried to help everyone who entered the court, as best as I could. Then I reminded him of his now ironic line about "we have to follow the rules."

Ultimately, I granted Officer Green's request and dismissed the ticket. The next week, I called the courteous clerk at the cemetery office and reported to him that I discussed customer service with the cemetery counsel. I asked him to see if the attorney would waive the $150 filing fee in this case. Two days later in a return call, I was advised the fee was excused, but only once as a "matter of courtesy".

# Chapter Eighteen

# The Boxer

*In the clearing stands a boxer,
And a fighter by his trade
And he carries the reminders
Of ev'ry glove that laid him down
Or cut him till he cried out
In his anger and his shame,
"I am leaving, I am leaving."
But the fighter still remains.*

<u>The Boxer</u>, by Paul Simon, 1968, Risa Song Lyrics Archive

---

Many world champion boxers like Marvin Hagler trained in local gyms. Muhammad Ali, then Cassius Clay, trained for his first heavyweight championship fight against the well-known Sonny Liston at the Petronelli Brothers 5th Street Gym in South Miami. The Main Street Gym in Los Angeles is where the great welterweight Roberto Duran trained for his big fight against Pepino Cuevas. The Kronk Gym, a training emporium for professional boxers, is located at the intersection of Warren and McGraw in the City of Detroit. The Kronk Gym was the home of World Champion Thomas Hearns

Hearns, who went by the fight name "The Hit Man", won numerous world titles in four different weight classes before ending his boxing career. He lost two of the most sensational boxing matches ever fought against "Marvelous" Marvin Hagler and "Sugar Ray" Leonard. Tommy had them both on the ropes before letting them get away in the final rounds. Kronk's leader was boxing visionary Emanuel "Manny" Steward, the famous trainer, promoter and TV announcer who handled many of the world champions.

Numerous colorful names in boxing history trained at Kronk. There was Milton McCrory and his little brother Stevie, an Olympic champ in his own right. Then there was Hilmar Kinty and Mickey "Sneaky Pea" Goodwin, a white, gifted all-around athlete from Melvindale High school. You may remember Leon Spinks who, with his brother Michael, won gold medals in the 1976 Olympics. Leon defeated Muhammad Ali for the heavyweight championship of the world one time. But wine, women and song ruined poor Leon's career. There were countless other boxers with big dreams, but short on the punching power needed to make a name in the fight game.

Some fighters stopped in at Kronk for a short time, just for the privilege of training under the watchful eye of Manny Steward. They were fighters such as Julio Cesar Chavez, Oscar DeLaHoya, and Evander Holyfield, a four-time heavyweight champion. In those "glory days" at the Kronk Gym, it was one amazing event after another, one amazing fight after another and numerous sideshows and soap operas in between.

The first time I heard of William "Caveman" Lee was in 1981, just before his upside down professional fight with John LoCicero. After being pounded early in the fifth round, amazingly the Caveman recovered his wits and won the fight with a knock out at the end of same round. Ring announcer Al Bernstein picked that round as one of the best fight rounds in boxing history. Later when Mickey Goodwin had to withdraw from a middleweight championship fight against Marvelous Marvin Hagler, Caveman agreed to fill in for him at the last minute and stepped into the ring. In the famous one-punch-first-round, Caveman received a shattering fist to his chin. He was down and out for the count.

From that point on in his career, things began going downhill for the Caveman. He was barely able to stay at Kronk as Tommy Hearn's sparring partner. This was at a time when Hearn's career was taking off like a rocket. Every day the Caveman sparred with Hearns, he took more and more shots to the head. Every night the Caveman took drugs to control the pain—trading the fog of the headshots for the fog of the drugs. As the accumulated punches took their toll, nothing in his head seemed to work very well. One day through this haze, he came up with an idea of making some easy money.

Caveman drove his car out of the Kronk Gym parking lot and north on Interstate I-75. He exited at Auburn Hills in northern Oakland County near the Palace of

Auburn Hills where he always dreamed of fighting the big fight. About a mile off the freeway, he entered the First Federal Savings and Loan bank in the Rochester Hills Professional Office Plaza building. Stepping through the glass entryway, he awkwardly told everyone there, "This is a stick up." The teller handed over some amount of money in a pre-packaged canvas bank bag with red dye secretly planted inside with the cash. The Caveman gingerly walked out, got into his car and tried to find his way back down Walton Boulevard to the interstate. The red dye pellets exploded, as they were designed, less than 100 yards from exiting the parking lot in front of the professional building. Word went out through the alarm systems alerting the police of the robbery. So many 911 calls came in from fellow drivers; the dispatcher was able to track the escape route, as if the cops had a "bear in the air". In an abandoned gas station near the interstate on-ramp, two officers waited for their lawbreaker to come into sight. Caveman was driving toward them with red dye smoke billowing out around his head stuck out the driver's window. What a spectacle! Seeing this sight, one of the officers said to the other, "Do you think we have the right car?"

Caveman was arrested without a struggle and taken to a holding cell in the county jail. He was locked up with many other hapless characters also swimming against the tide of life, waiting to be transported to one court or another. His arraignment on the armed robbery charge was scheduled for the next morning. While waiting in this crowded lockup, Caveman noticed the familiar face of Aram "Rocky" Alkazoff, who was in the same slammer waiting to be transferred to a federal prison. Rocky worked out at the Kronk in the Seventies. "Is that you Rocky?" Caveman said.

In despair, comfort comes in small unexpected ways. This chance meeting and conversation consoled each of them. Rocky described the conditions of the jail he was sitting in to his old acquaintance. This place is "as filthy, overcrowded, noisy, and as unfeeling a place as there is in this United States, the home of the free and the brave."

Rocky continued his expressive lament to the wide-eyed Caveman. "First of all you wear a pajama type outfit of green that is full of old sweat and smell, and all you have for your feet is these broken up slippers. Then the food is not fit for a human being and there is so little, that people fight for it. You get no fresh air, ever. The place is either too cold or too hot, and always noisy. There is nothing to read, the phones rarely work and maybe if you're lucky, you might get a shower. The mail hardly works, the sheriffs hardly do anything for you, no matter how polite you ask and you could go weeks without seeing a pencil or soap. You might get to watch an old television which hardly comes in because they don't allow antennas and you might get a torn up scrap of an old newspaper to read, if you're lucky.

"All you can do is sit on a steel block or bench, and just stare forward like a fool for hours at a time. In a holding cell, there is no water, no food and if you want to go to the bathroom, you have to do it in front of everybody. Never in your life will you feel so ashamed, hopeless and less than a human being than in one of these places, but you know me Caveman; I don't complain."

Other than Rocky, "the inmates were all black men with ages ranging from eighteen to over seventy. Everyone looked the same to the cops. The men were all skinny, underfed and most of them had crack cocaine habits. The hollow-eyed prisoners looked like they just stepped off the streets of desolation into cold turkey incarceration. Most of these guys were green with a long way to go. Even the older quieter guys looked terrible. Their faces said it all. It was obvious that before incarceration, these lost souls were out there in the free world living on a steady non-protein diet of drugs. For them, there was no food on the outside and really none to speak of on the inside either. A lot of the prisoners had sores, scars, and open abscesses from shooting up. They smelled. They all smelled." Caveman didn't feel good being there, but spending the afternoon in this hellhole with an old familiar face delighted him.

Caveman may have used some additional advice from the movie character Rocky Balboa, when he said: "The world ain't all sunshine and rainbows. It is a very rough mean place and no matter how tough you think you are, it will always bring you to your knees and keep you there permanently, if you let it. You or nobody ain't never gonna hit as hard as life. But it ain't about how hard you hit; it's about how hard you can get hit and keep moving forward. How much you can take and keep moving forward. If you know what you're worth, then go out and get what you're worth. But you gotta be willing to take the hit."

On the day of the preliminary exam, the courtroom was packed with spectators. When I arrived at the courthouse, I asked my court officer Tom to go into the courtroom and make sure the seating was properly handled. Emanuel Steward and his brother James, another Kronk regular, were given seats in the first row directly behind the defense table. The bind-over hearing was a forgone conclusion. A few witnesses were called to testify and provide the minimum facts necessary to establish the elements of armed robbery and probable cause to believe that Caveman was the looter of the savings and loan.

It took less than a half-day for the hearing. I bound the matter over to the circuit court for a jury trial and began to address the subject of bond. Every now and then circumstances may change since the original bond hearing where a prosecutor may want to ask the court to increase the amount of bond for one reason or another; especially where the facts indicate the likelihood of conviction is great or where the defendant may flee the jurisdiction of the court before the trial date. In these situations, a prosecutor sometimes asks the judge to increase the bond to an amount that will insure the defendant remains in the county jail until trial. The constitution requires a judge to set a reasonable bond in all cases, except in a first degree murder case. But reasonableness is a subjective concept on which practical minds are able to differ, so there is always a debate.

Caveman's bond was originally set at $500,000 cash. He was unable to post a bond of that amount. The assistant prosecutor knew the cash bond was sufficient to keep Caveman locked up and therefore he did not ask to increase the bond. If Caveman could afford a bond in this amount, he probably would not have committed the stick-up in the first place.

Just as the proceedings were concluding for the day, I stood up in my flowing black robe to leave the bench when a hand went up in the first row. Emanuel Steward said he wished to address the court. Many times in the past I entertained questions from visitors seated in the courtroom, especially during the bond hearing stage of the proceedings. Every so often parents or family members will want to speak on behalf of their loved ones and inform the court of special circumstances of the defendant being arraigned that might affect the amount of the bond.

I asked Mr. Steward to stand at the podium and place his name on the record. He was very recognizable from his many appearances on television boxing matches as a trainer and TV announcer. "Your Honor, as to the question of bond of Mr. Lee... I know this is a serious matter, but I would like to ask you to consider placing Mr. Lee on a temporary personal bond in my custody." The assistant prosecutor, although a great fan of boxing, could not believe what he was hearing. Here was a layman, in a highly uncharacteristic move, pleading before the bar and asking for custody of a defendant charged with a life felony. This request was coming from the mouth of Emanuel Steward, the mentor of all the uncharacteristic characters living in the world of flat-out destruction.

"Your Honor," Mr. Steward continued, studiously avoiding the use of the nickname 'Caveman'. "I need Mr. Lee. You see, Tommy Hearns has a major fight in Las Vegas in two weeks and I need Mr. Lee to go with us to Las Vegas in order to continue Tommy's training. I will bring Mr. Lee right back after the fight and give him back to you." Any assistant prosecutor would think that this is crazy. A personal bond is one thing, but no one is ever allowed to leave the state while waiting for trial on such a serious charge. Most judges will deny this type of a request. But I gave his request serious consideration. The idea of Caveman being an integral part of the Hearns championship fight intrigued me. My response was just as uncharacteristic as the request. Still standing at the bench, I ruled, "Here we have a boxer whose brains have been scrambled from being hit in the head too many times. Where is he to go if I release him? He could use a caretaker at no expense to the taxpayers. At least we will know where he is for the next couple of weeks, or so. Mr. Steward, he's all yours. But you will have to promise me you will bring him back after the fight."

The deputies from the jail, who are always around the courtroom to provide security in the building, had smiles on their faces as they witnessed this unusual event. Two and a half weeks later, Tommy Hearns won another world championship fight and the fallen Caveman was returned to custody in the county jail. The assistant prosecutor could now relax.

The Caveman was awaiting his rendezvous with justice and his upcoming trial. The groundbreaking Supreme Court case of *Gideon v Wainright*, established a constitutional guarantee that all criminal defendants have the right to be represented by a lawyer at all the stages of the proceedings, whether they can afford a lawyer or not. If any defendant is ever denied their constitutional right to a lawyer, it would constitute a denial of a fair trial. Anyone can waive their right to counsel and represent themself, but that option made no sense, even in Caveman's compromised brain. A trial is a war of words where the inarticulate are doomed to failure. Emanuel Steward again came to the rescue and took care of the whole lawyer problem. He hired one of his numerous attorney friends to represent the Caveman. Manny was there for Caveman, because Caveman was there for Manny and Tommy, when they needed him.

The Caveman was apprehensive, however. He had often boxed in public arenas before thousands of lunatic boxing fans. Now as he awaited trial, he shuddered at the thought of his trial being open to public display with all the witnesses telling their version of his botched adventure. How embarrassing. While Caveman didn't have much left, he still had his pride.

Caveman's attorney knew he had a right to raise an insanity defense at trial. Failure to consider the defense of insanity, especially in Caveman's case, would clearly be considered attorney malpractice. Caveman's attorney gave notice to the prosecutor before trial of his intention to raise an insanity defense. Based on that notification, the circuit judge ordered Caveman to be taken to the Center for Forensic Psychiatry in Ypsilanti, Michigan to undergo a mental examination for criminal responsibility. Just to cover his bases, Caveman's lawyer ordered an independent psychiatric exam for a second opinion. Consideration of the insanity defense was based on Caveman's professional career in the boxing ring suffering punishing blows to the head that could have killed a normal human being. At issue, with the repetitive blows to the head and the traumatic brain damage Caveman suffered, was his ability to know and appreciate the difference between right and wrong. Did he know the stick up was wrong, or alternatively, was Caveman able to resist the impulse to stick up the savings and loan? The law's "right/wrong" test and "irresistible impulse" test would be a question for the jury to decide, if Caveman actually pursued an insanity defense. Laugh, as you will at the insanity defense, a defense of last resort when you are caught really red handed; but the legitimacy of the insanity defense is well grounded in both the nature of our humanity and in our philosophy of the law.

For the Caveman, the insanity defense was not to be. Each examiner prepared a forensic psychiatric report and provided it to the prosecutor and Caveman's attorney. The defendant is presumed to be sane and therefore, the defendant has the burden to overcome that presumption, with expert psychological testimony indicating legal insanity. But in Caveman's case, neither psychiatric report overcame that presumption. Caveman was legally sane when he stuck up the savings and loan. Both parties reviewed the psychiatric reports and agreed to have a meeting with the circuit judge to discuss those results. No doubt the Caveman was suffering traumatic brain injury from a series of concussions and accumulated blows to the head, but he still had enough cognitive ability to know that robbing the savings and loan was wrong and he still had enough volitional ability to resist the impulse to rob the savings and loan because he was able to say "no" to the stick up temptation. An insanity defense was no longer in the cards for the Caveman.

Emanuel Steward wanted to come to court again and testify as to Caveman's good character. Caveman was a good man. He always arrived on time for work. Caveman never stole anything previously and he was very loyal and helpful to Manny. Caveman's character was not admissible in a trial, however, to prove whether he did or did not do one thing or another. Manny was just trying to help in any way he could. It all came down to the very week of trial when the attorneys were called in to meet with the trial judge one more time; to see if the case could be resolved short of trial. Cavemen had been in jail waiting for trial for about six months and by now the inhuman conditions inside the cell were starting to overwhelm him. Caveman needed to get out of the county jail and get a fresh start, even if it meant a change of scenery in Jackson Prison. He told his lawyer, if he was going to go to prison after the trial, he might as well get the best deal he could obtain before trial and get on with it. He knew the penitentiary had to be better than the county jail.

The trial circuit judge was in a good mood and took into consideration this was Caveman's first criminal offense, although it was a very serious infraction of the law. Caveman pled straight up to a lesser offense of unarmed robbery and was sentenced from 8 to 20 years in the state prison. That is a pretty good deal. Caveman was facing life or any number of years up to life in prison for the armed robbery charge. With this plea-bargain; he would be eligible for parole after serving five years.

Upon entering the plea, William "Caveman" Lee became a convicted felon. He lost everything he had at the Kronk Gym and was incarcerated in the state prison system for five years. When he finally got out of prison, his brains were even more scrambled. Emanuel Steward will claim his own spot in boxing history and William "Caveman" Lee will slide into obscurity, a forgotten man, his story preserved for the most part only on these pages.

**And then there is this...**

Emanuel Steward passed away October 25, 2012. At the memorial service Caveman Lee was in attendance for Manny to continue his close friendship in honor his "trainer". Also present was Shawn Windsor of the *Detroit Free Press* and he reported this:

"Emanuel Steward might not have saved William (Caveman) Lee's life, but giving Lee the keys to his house certainly helped.

"Never mind that Lee had held up three banks and had done time in prison. Or that Lee had thrown away his shot at the crown by ingesting morphine. Or that Lee hadn't stepped into a ring in any meaningful way in decades -- Lee offered Steward nothing in the way of a boxing future.

"If anything, Lee represented one of Steward's greatest misfires. The iconic boxing trainer regarded Lee as the hardest puncher he'd ever seen. Perhaps this explains why Lee was at Steward's memorial service Tuesday afternoon at Greater Grace Temple on Detroit's northwest side.

"Despite Lee's criminal past and wasted talent, Steward never gave up on him. In fact, Steward invited him down to Kronk to help keep kids from following the same path he did, which is what Lee had been doing until Steward's death.

"Steward sent Lee a plane ticket in the late 1970s and invited him to train and live here. Lee had grown up in Philadelphia, where he'd honed his style: a meat-grinding middleweight with hands that felt like stone.

"Though Lee tossed away all the natural talent -- he once fought Marvin Hagler and got knocked out in the first round because he was on morphine -- he has spent the past six years trying to make good on the promise in new ways. Since he was released from prison in 2006, Lee has worked as a security guard and a scrap metal gopher.

"It has been a tough life."

# Chapter Nineteen

# Sentencing

*City girls just seem to find out early*
*How to open doors with just a smile*
*A rich old man*
*And she won't have to worry*
*She'll dress up all in lace and go in style*

*So she tells him she must go out for the evening*
*To comfort an old friend who's feelin' down*
*But he knows where she's goin' as she's leavin'*
*She is headed for the cheatin' side of town*

*You can't hide your lyin' eyes*
*And your smile is a thin disguise*
*I thought by now you'd realize*
*There ain't no way to hide your lyin eyes*

*Lyin' Eyes* The Eagles, Glenn Frey and Don Henley, 1972

---

In the first few years of private practice, the courtroom was often my classroom. On Motion days, I sat in many of these courtrooms and listened to the proceedings all the while supposing how I would rule on the same facts, if I were the sitting judge. This is a great exercise, not only to sharpen the legal mind, but also to discern how the same particular judge may rule should I present a similar argument in his or her courtroom.

Judges' rulings come in countless times during hearings and trials, especially rulings on the admissibility of evidence. Each case must come to its own conclusion at some point in time, especially criminal cases; the final ruling is referred to as the Sentencing of the defendant by the judge. Judges have had, in the past, unfettered discretion to sentence one to any amount of fine or any number of years of imprisonment up to the maximum of the appropriate statute. Today, however, governing bodies have created sentencing guidelines for most all criminal offences, setting a range of penalties that can be imposed for each offense. All judges are required to sentence within these guidelines. If a defendant commits multiple crimes, the sentencing judge can order the terms of each offense to be additive, meaning a Consecutive Sentence or all the terms may be consolidated and served together as one, meaning a Concurrent Sentence.

The Honorable James S. Thorburn was a wily and wonderful man from whom to learn the law. He held fort daily in his second floor courtroom in the circuit court building. As a very experienced lawyer, Judge Thorburn was always well prepared and seemed to enjoy the verbal combat with those lawyers who came before his bench. He had no problems in resolving disputes in unique ways. Practicing lawyers trusted him and many times would wave their criminal client's right to a jury trial and opt for a Judge Thorburn hearing of the facts and law without a jury. When defendants were, in his opinion, overcharged in criminal matters, he did not hesitate in finding the defendant guilty of a lesser offense or even dismissing the case altogether, after considering all the testimony. I would describe his style as gentle, but firm.

In one interesting case, I was first assigned to represent a defendant charged with the offense of Armed Robbery. Within the City of Royal Oak, Michigan, sits a Catholic church named The Shrine of the Little Flower. The church is named after the French Saint Therese de Lisieux, known as the Little Flower; a Carmelite nun who died from tuberculosis at the age of 25 in 1897. It was the same parish where controversial Fr. Charles Coughlin made Sunday radio pro-Hitler speeches during World War II, until such time when he was silenced by the Catholic Church in Rome. One Sunday my defendant stalked and waited outside the church building until the conclusion of the last Sunday mass before entering the sacristy and depriving the church of their entire Sunday collections.

At the first court hearing after the defendant was arrested and arraigned, about ten days later, the testimony about the robbery was presented to a local District Judge. Everything was clear except for the fact that the police failed to advise my client of many of his legal rights upon arresting him. I made a perfunctory motion to dismiss the case because of a legal decision in an old case named *People v. White*. Along with the prosecutor and the police involved in the investigation,

I was shocked when the judge granted my motion, dismissed the case and released my client without bond. This meant he was free to go wherever he pleased. My job as appointed defense attorney was complete; however, I advised my just-freed client to leave the state before the police re-issued the complaint and warrant and re-arrested him.

As predicted, the charges were re-written and my cocky client, who thought he knew better, was re-arrested and taken back into custody. Judge Thorburn thought I had done too good a job on the first round in court and said that he would not re-appoint me to represent this defendant, lest I gain his freedom a second time. Another attorney was appointed and the case moved to the jury trial stage, while all along the defendant remained in custody. After the jury was impanelled, Judge Thorburn, in his inimitable bravura and not wanting to waste his time on a long trial, counseled with the newly appointed defense attorney. He warned him that for each and every day the trial continues, the defendant will receive an additional sentence of twenty years in prison—a significant increase of time to serve, since the offense of Armed Robbery carried a maximum sentence of up to any number of years in prison. The judge had hoped this discussion would cause the defendant to enter a plea and forgo the need for a trial. But that was not to happen. The trial lasted three days before the jury convicted the church heister of the armed robbery charge and the defendant was, as promised, sentenced to a term of 60 to 80 years in the state prison system. This type of coercive sentencing would clearly be cause for a reversal by an appeals court in this day and age.

*****

Subsequent to becoming District Judge in the same county, Judge Thorburn and I drifted apart. We still remained friends throughout the years and enjoyed meeting up with each other at various judge's dinners and seminars. My court had a very small probation department with one probation officer assigned to provide pre-sentence evaluations when needed. She was the best in the business. We did not need additional personal. Like Judge Thorburn, I had over ten years' experience in all the courts in the area before taking the bench. I knew just about what I wanted to do when sentencing someone because of the repetition of similar cases. For example: the district court handled most of the drinking and driving cases as proscribed by state law. That law also specified the limitation on the type of sentence one could receive. The experienced judges were very consistent with their sentencing in this area of the law. Over the years, nevertheless, the simple matter of sentencing began to take on a new appearance.

Various social groups with their own agenda, such as MADD (Mothers Against Drunk Drivers), became prominent and hard-pressed their influence on the community and the judges, who needed the public on their side for purposes of reelection. Simple matters as the management of court cases often became micromanaged unintentionally. With that, it became necessary for the probation department to be expanded to cover their increased duties. Every convicted defendant now needed to be screened and followed with a pre-sentence report, unlike formerly when judges shot from the hip. The Michigan State Police began keeping elaborate records on drunken driving convictions and the statistics of how each judge sentenced defendants in their court. More paperwork!

Newer and younger judges were elected, as time moved on, each with his or her specific political agendas. One court in the southern part of the county was served by three younger judges who decided amongst themselves they were going to stamp out drunk driving in their own community. They decided that all drinking and driving defendants would receive a sentence to some amount of time in jail, anywhere from 3 to 7 days, just to prove their point. Unfortunately no judge can create or set his or her own minimum sentence, because the state laws allow for probation without a jail term as the minimum sentence.

The population in my district grew rapidly due to the healthy economy and residential growth to about 180,000 which necessitated new additional judges. They were younger and from the new school of thought. I sensed that they believed I was more liberal in my sentencing and indicated their feelings by being "tough on crime" in their own sentencing style. A couple of years after the state police began collecting and compiling their data on drunken driving sentencing, they released their public records which showed that I was the second toughest sentencing judge in the county. I knew that these figures would eventually be released sometime in the future, probably during the next election cycle. So from the outset, I refashioned my sentencing orders to take into consideration the information in which the police were interested. While my sentencing style did not change, the manner in which it was reported changed and, as a result, the final figures placed my court near the top, to the shock of my fellow judges.

Everyone should be treated fairly and equally by the court. Most people, except for a few defendants, were never familiar with my special annual Christmas gift. Each year during the week before Christmas, at the height of the shopping season, I check the county jail roster to see if any inmates were still incarcerated because of my sentencing. Quietly, I sent an Order over to the Sheriff releasing those of mine from jail the day before Christmas. A simple gesture fitting with the season!

The Sixties was the era of the hippies and Timothy Leary. They spawned children with equal complaints against society called hipsters, those who rejected the established culture of governance and refused to be bound by existing authority. One such character was Brian Stuart. One day he appeared in my court responding to a minor traffic ticket along with a companion ticket for not possessing a valid Michigan driver's license. He proceeded to get my attention by lecturing me on how the State had no right to tell him what to do. He said he was a person of the world and not subject to the driver's license rules. I patiently listened to his diatribe. It was near the end of the day and all I wanted to do was go home. I thanked him for his discussion and told him I did not want to see him back in this court again without a valid driver's license.

The next time I saw Brian was again in the courtroom in a felony case where he and his younger brother Eric were charged with interference with a police officer in the performance of his duty. It seems his brother Eric parked their auto on Lake Orion when the lake was frozen over. Brother Eric involved himself in an argument with the sheriff's deputy when he was told to remove the car from the lake surface. Brian came to his brother's defense and a scuffle between the deputy and Eric ensued. Both brothers were arrested and taken to jail. It was a sad scene when Brian arrived in court for his preliminary hearing. He was led into the courtroom with full casts on both of his arms. He apparently opened his mouth one too many times and harangued the wrong person in the jail lock-up. That guy responded by breaking both of Brian's arms. There is a lesson somewhere in there.

The hearing began and witnesses were called to testify. Brian did not slow down from his recent experience in the jail. He continued his outbursts in the court; interrupting the witness' testimony. I ordered the court officer to remove Brian from the courtroom, creating peace and quiet. At the end of the hearing, after all of the testimony was taken, I ruled that Brian was not a participant in the fracas with the officer and did not touch him, but only exercised his right to free speech, all be it, unruly and hard to take. Brian became an unforgettable character.

Fast forward, in your mind, to the few weeks before I retired from the bench and left office. There before my very eyes appeared Brian Stuart with that mischievous smirk on his face. He received another driving on a suspended license and driving without a license on person ticket. His attitude said to me, "What are you going to do about these tickets this time?" We proceeded to discuss our previous encounters and my persistent admonitions that he not drive without obtaining a driver's license from the state. He continued with his confrontational rage about his beliefs in freedom from government. I knew I would no longer be around to further educate Mr. Stuart by gentle persuasion. Brian was found guilty of these misdemeanors and immediately sentenced to ninety days flat out in the Oakland County Jail. Hopefully Brian learned his lesson and got the message. He was released from jail sometime after I retired and moved from the area.

## And then there is this...

The other day I viewed a video from StarGazette.com, a Gannett Company Video Network, reporting on a Cleveland woman sentenced for driving her auto down the public city sidewalk in order get around a stopped school bus. The local judge sentenced the driver to public admonishment—wearing a sign around her neck saying "only an idiot would drive on the sidewalk to avoid a school bus."

Justifying the sentence, the judge said the driver did not show any remorse and she deserved more than a fine. The driver, in the video, stood in shame for the afternoon wearing the sign.

There are few guidelines for misdemeanor sentencing. Basically the statues and ordinances set the maximum of a fine and allow for a maximum time in jail in specific cases from 30 to 90 days. Often judges in minor cases like to consider a short period of community service, such as volunteer work at the church.

Early on in my judgeship around the Thanksgiving and Christmas season, I ordered high school students, who would later have their cases dismissed, to donate canned goods to the local food bank as part of their sentence. On its face, there was a humanitarian aspect to this project. It was my though the youths would go home, speak with their parents and take canned food from their own cupboards for those donations. I soon found, however, that these teen rascals quickly found their way to the A&P Store close to the court and purchased cases of soup or vegetables and delivered it directly to the food bank. Not much of a sacrifice, I thought later. The store called my office and asked that I cut back on these sentences. They were running short of canned inventories.

I call sentences like this "do-good sentences". I later came to believe this type of sentencing was not the role of the court, *vis-a-vis* aiding the local charitable groups around town. It is so easy to create the appearance of impropriety while trying to do something worthy for the community. I discontinued specific programs and turned those details to our probation officers who worked closely with the judges. They have the pulse of the community and are able to follow up with those on probation.

# Chapter Twenty
# The Jury and the Pub

*"To laugh often and love much;
to win the respect of intelligent persons and the affection of children ...
to appreciate beauty;
to find the best in others;
to give of one's self;
to leave the world a bit better ...
to have played and laughed with enthusiasm and sung with exultation;
to know even one life has breathed easier because you have lived ...
This is to have succeeded."*

Ralph Waldo Emerson

---

Extraordinary times sometimes call for extraordinary measures in order to bring things back to normal. I inherited a considerable backlog of cases in my first year on the bench. To solve this concern, I developed my version of the one-day-one-trial jury selection procedure. Generally speaking, the public is hesitant to take the time out of their busy schedules to sit in a court and listen to another's problems. Yet, we can all agree that jury duty is a noble public service and the responsibility of all citizens. It probably does not surprise you the many ways citizens try to avoid being picked for jury duty. It is true, as some say, the jury selection process is as important as the trial itself. All cases rise or fall on the shoulders of the jury panel selected.

In the State of Michigan, all licensed drivers are eligible for jury duty. Years ago, only registered voters were summoned by the courts to become prospective jurors. The change to using registered drivers resulted in a substantial increase in the number of jurors in the pool. In smaller jurisdictions, some poor souls received jury notices every year. That process just makes for hostile jurors. I took the jury selection process as an opportunity to interact with the residents of the community and inform them how my court works. My prospective jurors were requested to be present at the courthouse at 2pm on Friday afternoon one week a month. They were told the jury trials would take place during the next week and, if they were not selected as jurors, they would be free to go home with no additional obligation to the court during this term. On the other hand, selected jurors would be asked to return to court one day in the next week.

"My name is Judge Sheehy and I am so pleased you were able to make it down to court today. I will try to use as little of your time as possible. I know all of you have busy schedules, but I'm sure sitting as jurors will be an exciting experience." The new jurors were not always soothed by my simple introduction. To some, this is not the type of excitement they had in mind. One day after greeting a new group of jurors, I looked to the back of the jury assembly room and saw a mother nursing her new baby. She told me she had no babysitter or anyone in her family with whom to leave her child. This was a first, but I took it in stride and thanked the lady for stopping by the court and excused her. This kind gesture in front of the other jurors seemed to please them. They saw the understanding side of the judge, a side not often apparent by the regular court customers.

As the jurors began to assemble for the selection process, lawyers and litigants try to settle their cases during the preceding hour in the courtroom and hallways. Some attorneys will always need to talk to the judge. The secret of keeping all the balls in the air at the same time is having a competent staff to facilitate and interact with everyone's needs. Tom Cattel was the court officer for the previous judge and knew the ways of the legal system. He stayed on with me when I joined the court. We hit it off and worked well together. Tom had been a police officer before retiring and coming to work with the court. He had the greatest attitude and was an expert in handling street people. One day a homeless man stepped into the courtroom with everything he owned strapped to his back. Tom greeted him as if he were his prodigal son. Tom slipped the table leg out of his backpack as he gave him a big hug and said, "Let me hang on to this until you leave." Tom had a wonderful sense of humor. He kept everyone in the building laughing with the one-liners he brought to work every morning. One day the courtroom was filled with consumers waiting for a session of court to open and the judge to take the bench. Tom entered the courtroom first, in essence to warm up the crowd. He said to all in a questioning manner, "Has anyone seen an orange Titleist (golf ball) roll through here?" All in the room had smiles on their faces and court was ready to begin.

Tom lined up all the attorneys that needed to speak with the judge. As I returned to my chambers after greeting the jury array, Tom switched positions and joined the waiting jurors. He humored them with stories from his police department days. The jury schedule was light this particular month. Only six cases were set for trial the next week. The first lawyer in line to see me settled his case with a plea to a reduced charge and only needed to know if I would extend the time his client had to pay the fine. Along the same lines, the second defense attorney needed to know if I was inclined to send his client to jail. Each case needed some of my personal attention. Finally, two cases remained for jury selection—one civil and one criminal.

Tom led the thirty or so jurors down the back hallway and into the courtroom. Jurors are selected by random numerical draw. Their personal names are never used for their own safety and protection. Jurors' numbers 6, 12, 23, 2, 17 and 8 were called and they took their place in the jury box. A few preliminary questions are asked by the court and then the attorneys have a chance to ask the jurors questions. This part of the selection process is called the *vois dire*, from Latin derivation meaning "saying the truth (*verum dicere*)." Attorneys usually want to find out from the prospective jurors, through the questions they ask, if any have preconceived opinions or prejudices about the subject of the lawsuit. If a prospective juror has aversion towards alcohol, for example, he or she most likely would not be objective enough to sit on a drunken driving case. A juror may be excused "for cause", which is a prejudice or position they may express and which becomes obvious to all. In addition, an attorney may excuse two or three jurors for no reason at all; these are called "preemptory challenges". The two juries were selected and seated. The first trial would begin Monday morning at 9 am sharp. The second trial was set to start Wednesday.

Monday morning was a beautiful warm sunlit day. Out behind the courthouse near the city hall, senior citizens gather to feed the ducks in the pond. Some will sit and feed the fowl for an hour or so, before walking over to the court to watch what is going on. These folks are referred to as the "regulars". The jurors are asked to show up to court a little before nine when the court staff likes to prepare coffee and rolls for them. Tom walked into my office to tell me only five of the six selected jurors arrived this morning. One called in and said she was sick and could not be present. I needed six jurors and looked out my window as an idea came to me. I pointed towards the pond and asked Tom to go outside and ask one of the "regulars" to fill in on this jury panel. When court began, a few minutes later, six jurors were sworn in and the trial began with jury instructions and opening statements by the attorneys.

Across the street and down a little from the courthouse is a pleasant and friendly neighborhood tavern. The jurors want to know where they can go for lunch. They are always told the Pub was a great place to have their lunch, because it was close by and it had great food. It is called The Hamlin Pub, named that by its owner Al George. He was a long time tavern keeper and this Pub was the fifth watering hole he operated. The Hamlin Pub was situated in a strip mall, in a spot where a beer and wine store had just closed. Al figured, with the courthouse close by, he could make a go of it in this location. As it turned out, the world's greatest host was correct. From day one, the Pub was packed with customers from the lunch hour through closing.

The police always like to keep a lid on new bars by sticking their collective noses into the owner's business. In this case it was the sheriff's department and specifically the midnight shift deputies who patrolled the streets around the Pub going out of their way to harass the Pub. Al started receiving complaints from his customers about being stopped within a few blocks, after leaving the Pub late at night. The sheriff's deputies lit up the night with their blue lights, stopping a good number of bar folks.

Al came over to the courthouse and asked to see me. He talked about this intrusion into his business by the deputies and we finally came up with a plan. One night during the next week around one-fifteen in the morning, a customer staggered out of the Pub and got into his car. He pulled out of the parking lot and made a left turn. Within less than a city block, a deputy in a marked patrol car pulled the patron over. The deputy asked the motorist for his license and insurance and went on to give him a state approved data-master breath test. To the deputy's surprise, the meter read 0.00. The deputy asked the driver, "Didn't you just come out of the Pub." The answer was "Yes sir." Confused, the deputy said the driver looked at first as if he were drunk. The driver responded, "Deputy, I am the designated decoy. Since you stopped me over here, those remaining customers in the Pub left by the side door and drove away in the other direction." The driver was allowed to leave without receiving a ticket. The next day, Al contacted the captain at the sheriff's substation and invited all the deputies over to his bar. The next shift-change party was held at The Hamlin Pub and Al donated two large platters of *hors d'orves* to the cause. The Pub and Al no longer had any problems with deputies stopping customers at closing time.

Al and I began to get to know each other a little better. I realized I knew Al's wife Peggy from grade school at St. Scholastica's parish. Now we had something in common. I began stopping by the Pub after work a couple of times a week getting to know the customers. Like the seniors that visited my courtroom from the park, I realized the Pub had its own "regulars" who were sitting in the same seats every time I walked in. They all had their own stories. Scottie, a retired truck driver, was a loyal member of the Masonic Order. Frank was formerly employed as an operative for the Central Intelligence Agency. He could not understand why I never carried a pistol under my robes. Frank always wanted to talk about guns with me. He once invited me out to a firing range, so he could teach me how to shoot. One day I was pulled aside by another "regular" and quietly advised not to go shooting with Frank. He implied that Frank was still hearing noises in his head from his undercover days and he could be dangerous.

Johnny was a special trip and a man of multiple personalities all wrapped up in one package. He played college football before he became a professional boxer. After his boxing days, Johnny made a career as a bouncer in various bars around town. Johnny would also get calls to help out with security, when stars from the entertainment world came into town to perform. To say Johnny has a drink now and then is the world's greatest understatement. Johnny had a serious drinking problem. At first, I did not know Johnny was a drinker, until one day I ran into him on the street. He seemed different to me... he was sober. Johnny was usually half in the bag.

Johnny worked at many famous restaurants/bars like the Apollo Lounge, Joe Bathey's and the Club Cliché. Along the way, Johnny became a friend of Big John, a well-known and legendary tough guy on the Detroit saloon circuit. Johnny watched the back of Big John, who was a ladies man, a loyal friend and a guy who stepped aside for no one. One night at the Apollo, Big John ran into Raymond Rea, known as Ray-Ray in the world of head bangers. They both carried on a long-time personal grudge match. Ray-Ray always carried a snub nosed handgun for his own protection. A single shot rang out throughout the Apollo. It missed Big John and Johnny, but took down the bartender. Two days later, the bartender died from his wounds. That was the last time Johnny and Big John hung out together. Life is a risk, but it need not be tested every day. Johnny's days of bouncing in the famous bars were over and he now called The Hamlin Pub his home.

Near the courthouse was a neighborhood of residential homes set nicely among eighteen holes of a semi-public golf course. Christopher Wilhoit's home abutted the sixth hole. He invited his good friend and tavern owner Al George over for Sunday night dinner. They started out the evening with a few drinks on the back patio, while cooking steaks on the grill. Every now and then golf balls will find their way onto Wilhoit's back lawn. He and Al though it would be cute to take the garden hose out and spray golfers with water when they came into the yard looking for their wayward shots. Some of the sprayed golfers this day called the police and a young, inexperienced deputy appeared later that evening at Chris Wilhoit's front door. By that time, the boys were well into their grilled steaks and further into the infamous bottle. The deputy only wanted a statement about the alleged water assault. Chris was unable to articulate any thoughts by that time and slammed his front door in the face of the deputy.

The next time I saw Mr. Wilhoit was in my courtroom. The deputy issued to him an assault ticket on behalf of the golfer. I ordered the golfer into court to tell his side of the watering story before I would allow the ticket to go to trial. The golfer was an easygoing sort of guy and showed up to talk with me about ten days later. I sensed the golfer was over his bad feeling towards Wilhoit, who he never met; so I suggested the ticket would be held in limbo for six months and dismissed if Chris Wilhoit could behave himself. Later that afternoon, when I stopped by The Hamlin Pub, I announced my disposition of the assault ticket. The "regulars" gave me a standing ovation and let out a loud cheer. Chris Wilhoit bought me one of those large 24 oz. beers.

# Chapter Twenty-One
# Try Mediation

*Women tell about the "Glass Ceiling" experience in their careers. My wife was very successful as a professional woman, but I hear her discuss the glass ceiling with our daughter, the university professor. When I began the practice of law, all the circuit judges were male and most of the practicing bar from my perspective was male. Over the years, I witnessed what many still refer to as discrimination of women in general and with certain women specifically.*

*I met a number of the nicest and toughest ladies along the way. They needed to be strong and confident to stay floating above the water line. As the number of women judges increased, my style of practice adapted to the change. I recall in one court setting where my opposing counsel, a fine lady, addressed the court first, "Good morning your honor...You have a nice new haircut since we were here last week." Judge Alice responded, "Why thank you, dear. That is a very lovely suit you have on today. The colors fit nicely with the spring weather we are having."*

*This bald-headed stocky lawyer sat down and kept his mouth shut. I realized right then I was out-manned by the two ladies, even before the opening arguments. Clearly the practice of law took a discernible turn that day.*

---

At the start of my judicial career the docket had a bogged down backlog of cases. I had to learn how to run the scheduling of cases in an efficient manner, yet at the same time, provide those wishing to resolve disputes through their right to trial a reasonable amount of time to prepare their cases. Waiting for five years to conduct a civil trial is unacceptable. I tried to run the most effective court docket in the state. Often times, the only objection came from attorneys whose cases arrived on the trial list sooner than they were ready to begin. One would think that lawyers should better prepare their cases. However, it is clear that sufficient time must be allotted for discovery and preparation before opening a trial.

I signed up and attended The National Judicial College at the University of Nevada where special courses were offered towards the certification in the field of Mediation. The docket I inherited was simply out of control. My predecessor enjoyed not working full days...everyday, which created a logjam of Herculean proportions. The civil jury docket was backlogged in the range of two hundred cases. Similarly, the criminal jury docket was held up in the same manner, depriving many citizens of their right to a speedy trial. I worked hard to reduce this serious organizational problem. Of the many methods used to resolve the cases, some included my unique style of mediation. It seemed to me the large variety of cases had to be resolved in different ways based on their complexities, potential length and the relationships of the parties involved. The bottleneck cleared after eighteen months of creative scheduling.

A civil case, as an example, was filed by an Italian concrete forms dealer against an Italian cement contractor. One dealer claimed the other contractor used the forms for a longer period than he agreed and failed to return the correct number of the forms he was given. It was clear to me without a written contract; this case would become a real "he said—she said" argument, just short of physical confrontation. I picked up the telephone and called a high school classmate. I asked him if his retired father, an Italian contractor of thirty-five years, would come over to the courthouse and help these gentlemen settle their dispute. The next Wednesday, the two concrete litigators joined the retired contractor in the jury room and discussed a settlement of their dispute. Two hours later the case was resolved while I remained in the courtroom hearing other cases. The concrete contractor was not immediately happy with the results, but some months later he returned to the court with another lawsuit and thanked me for forcing the earlier settlement. The resolution saved everybody money and time.

Throughout the country, disputes are handled and resolved by a process called Mediation. True Mediation is a controlled process of assisting litigants or parties reach their own solution to their own dispute through the use of specific techniques or skills which improve communications and the understanding of each other's position. Litigants are usually happy with and more accepting of settlements they have a hand in creating.

Steven L. Schwartz, an attorney in Southfield, Michigan described the congested court problem. "Many judges feel as though they have become administrators forced to be more concerned with the movement of congested court dockets rather than dispensing justice. As for clients, they too see the system as hostile with delay, expense and uncertainty making the victor frequently indistinguishable from the vanquished." He went on to suggest the solution. Mediation "brings about a more non-adversarial, problem solving and interest-based approach to representing clients ... an environment is created in which most cases can be resolved cheaper, faster and with less destruction to personal and business relationships." And that is because, Mediation "is the concept that changes the framework for settling differences to working the common ground rather than in bunkers of positions and differences— the practical methodology by which we make this change."

Litigants do not understand the process of the courtroom. They also have no control of the outcome of a case and most often suffer the loss of time and money. Mediation, on the other hand, is a private voluntary dispute resolution process in which a mediator, selected by all of the parties, assists the disputants by identifying the issues of mutual concern, developing options for resolving those issues and finding resolutions. The benefit of mediating a settlement over trying a case in the courtroom setting is that the process is confidential and parties control their own outcome. Matters in dispute are resolved faster with less expense and there seems to be greater compliance with the accepted outcome, than with the judicial process.

In some cases, mediation benefits both sides, especially where a defendant has no hope of winning in court where delay is his best friend. A case in point is *Infinger v. Fidelity Group and Taylor Agency, Inc.* The Infinger family purchased a homeowner's insurance policy from the Taylor Agency, Inc. Infinger had a fire loss in their home during the policy period and suffered property damage amounting to $36,000. When Infinger filed their insurance claim at the Taylor Agency, Inc., they were told for the first time that no insurance policy was ever written because the Fidelity Group Insurance Company was never authorized to do business by the state insurance commissioner. The parties agreed to mediate the dispute before the case went to trial. The mediator explained the process and the mediation began in one of their lawyer's conference rooms. The position of the Infinger family was clear. They paid the full premium for the policy and expected their loss be completely covered by the insurance company. The insurance agent took the position that there was no insurance, but he offered to return the insurance premium paid by the Infinger family. Each party intractably clung to their respective positions after an hour and a half of discussions. The mediator's role is to keep the parties at the table and keep them talking. In this case however, he felt the mother and daughter Infinger needed a break and suggested they have a cup of coffee in the lounge down the hall.

Any discussion a mediator has with either party while alone and out of the presence of other is always confidential and not revealed to the other party without their permission. Sometimes topics of discussion are suggested to one party or the other. Here the mediator needed to get the insurance people off dead center so they could further discuss resolving the case with the homeowners. The mediator, a former prosecutor in his early years of practicing law, gained the attention of the insurance agency people by explaining to them some of the state's criminal laws. He told the Taylor Agency that they violated the law by selling what could be referred to as a "blue sky" contract; not worth the paper they are written on. The insurance people became more interested in listening.

When the Infingers returned to the conference room to continued discussions, the mediator tried a new technique. He excused himself to use the rest room and left all the parties alone in the room to talk among themselves. The mediator returned to the room in roughly ten minutes. Everyone announced they had come to an agreement to settle the case with a cash payment from the insurance agency to the Infingers in the amount of $28,000.

The mediation process follows a structured procedure. Upon conclusion, a written Settlement Agreement is always prepared. Parties are frequently anxious to leave as soon as they have reached an agreement. Writing and reviewing the final agreement is very important because it is the only evidence the parties will have to detail their settlement. Neither the mediator nor his records may be subpoenaed into court. The Settlement Agreement is an enforceable contract. This case was now settled. The Infingers were happy and no one became any wiser about the potential criminal behavior of the defendants.

Mediation can be used in cases that involve issues other than monetary damages. In the case of *Brewer and Bailey v. Lakefront Village Community*, a group of five homeowners filed a lawsuit seeking an injunction preventing the general public from having access or using the beach and waters in front of their homes. The community of homes was built on large lots in accordance to a subdivision plot plan. The property line of the residential lots abutting the lake was drawn in a straight line along the water's edge. Over the years, the water line receded and shifted allowing dry land between the homeowner's property line and the water's edge. This phenomenon allowed the unintended access and use of the beaches in front of those homes by others in the community, as if it were a public beach. A mediator was selected and the five homeowners and board of the homeowner's association arrived in the mediator's office. Everyone knew each other and enjoyed each other's company. The mediator conducted the meeting by controlling who would be able to speak and for how long. One lady poured coffee for all and kept it hot during the meeting. This is what the mediator called a "time" meeting. On a Saturday morning all the homeowners were happy to get together and have some coffee. By eleven-thirty many started looking at their watches, anxious to get out and do other things. By then, the respective parties were separated into two conference rooms and the talking became louder and more serious. The mediator shuttled back and forth, helping everyone stay focused on the pertinent issues. It took only an additional forty-five minutes for an agreement to be formulated. The homeowner's association agreed to have a land surveyor redo the plot plans, so as to move the lot lines further into the water precluding public access to the private lake.

However it was not over yet. The final issue was the payment of the costs to survey and change the plot plan. Voices got louder threatening to sink the original agreement. The mediator would not allow anyone to leave the building until this issue was resolved. One hour later, a compromise fee agreement came out of both rooms and everyone was released to go about their regular Saturday business. The pressure of time often serves to resolve the disputed issues.

Mediation not always results in a successful outcome. Keeping an open mind with the intention of compromise is a critical ingredient to a fruitful mediation. In the case, *Bank One v. Sky Star & Page*, William Page became an entrepreneur and opened a video rental store in a neighborhood strip mall. He took out a loan from Bank One, an Ohio Bank, in the amount of $200,000 in order to purchase the latest movies on VCR tape for his inventory. As sometimes happens to a small businessperson, lightning struck not once but twice, causing his business to falter. All of Page's video formats were eight-track cassette tapes. In the first six months the medium in the movie rental industry began to change from eight-track tape to the DVD format. Within a year all the new movies for his rentals were only available in the DVD format requiring Page to revamp his movie inventory. Also to his dismay, a new large Blockbuster store opened less than two blocks away. Page slowly lost his customers and started missing his loan payments. Bank One instituted this lawsuit after three month of default to recover their loan. The case went to mediation before trial.

The mediation started with discussions in an upbeat fashion and slowly they went downhill for the next two hours. The issues were pretty clear. Page owed the money; so just how much would the bank agree to accept in settlement?  Page absurdly took the position that the bank made a bad loan and they should share in Page's business misfortune and forgive the loan.  Banks are not venture capitalists; they make loans.  Page's common sense and business acumen was certainly challenged once again.  The mediator needed to be patient as the discussions developed.  He spoke privately with Page's attorney during a coffee break.  The lawyer just shrugged his shoulders when he was asked to get his client's head back into the ballgame.  The bank's final and most reasonable offer of settlement was for Page to agree to a civil judgment at $150,000, with a fixed interest amount and the bank would wave all the remaining interest and expenses of $100,000.   Page and his lawyer went behind closed doors and discussed this offer for twenty-five minutes.  When the closed door opened, Page still had no intention of paying anything.  The mediation was unsuccessful.

Some lawyers use the mediation process for discovery purposes and additional billing time, instead of trying to settle the case at hand.  *Angela Simon v. MBUSA* was such a case.  MBUSA was a large farm with a horse stable and training business.  They sold a ten-acre parcel of land at the end of their property to Angela Simon.  Ms. Simon was able to access her property by using a dirt road that came along MBUSA's main driveway.  Within a year, MBUSA made some changes to their business layout, which blocked off the dirt road Simon used to access her property. In many states it is against the law to sell landlocked real property without proper right of entry. Here the apparent entrance road was closed and Simon was unable to use her property. Additional parties were involved in the lawsuit such as the bank, the title company and the horsemen's association. Five lawyers participated in the mediation. Every time the mediator moved the discussions around the table, a new problem arose and each lawyer offered a different rational and solution. It was easy for one to become dizzy, after hours of discussions. It became obvious the MBUSA attorney had no intention of settling this case before trial. The mediator prepared his exit strategy and slowly brought the mediation to a conclusion. The litigants all agreed to meet again before the trial date. The mediator had no further interest in rehashing the same old facts of this case any further.

The mediation process is a great way to resolve pending litigation, if the parties are sincere and follow the mediator's directions to the end—settlement.

**And then there is this...**
On the quadrennial Election Day, 2012, I spent the day (14 ½ hours) working as a poll manager herding more than a thousand local neighbors through the labyrinth of wickets to cast their vote for the various elected offices in the state and national government.

Every Election Day reminds me of all the years when I needed to run for office first to earn my judgeship and later to retain it. I fondly remember my friends and associates who took the time to stand in all types of weather at the polls and hand out political flyers encouraging a vote for Judge Jim.

One year, I was opposed by a friend and lawyer by the name of John Katsoulis from Lakeville, Michigan. On that Election Day, I followed the usual routine to head out to all the polls and thank those covering and shake hands with as many voters as possible. Customarily lunch with my wife followed when we drove to Lake Orion and Gus' Steak House. Danny Vanelli, the proprietor, served up a fine steak sandwich as we just sat back to enjoy the day.

On the ride home, I noticed a small Piper Cub type plane overhead pulling a streamer saying "Elect John Katsoulis District Judge." I had a funny feeling that my opponent was really serious about winning. I asked Katy if she knew the number for an Air Force interceptor to take the down the opposition. There was no need for such drastic action though, as the electors took care of things. At the re-election party later that evening another victory was announced.

# Chapter Twenty-Two
# Walk Straight

*The military draft boards were very active during the late sixties and early seventies. The war in Vietnam roared like a hot fire, stoked by the ineptness of President Lyndon B. Johnson. Congress approved the Gulf of Tonkin Resolution in August of 1964 in response to two alleged minor naval skirmishes off the coast of North Vietnam. This Resolution gave the president power to conduct military operations in Southeast Asia without declaring war. "The Gulf of Tonkin Incident", writes Louise Gerdes, "is an oft-cited example of the way in which Johnson misled the American people to gain support for his foreign policy in Vietnam." The US soldiers paid the ultimate sacrifice however, with the loss 58,159 lives.*

---

Brian Nelson left his home in the Detroit area for the Vietnam Theater just about the same time I graduated from law school and began to practice law. I did not know him then, nor could I imagine how our paths would cross years later. During his tour of duty, Brian was a platoon leader assigned to the infantry. As such, he was also responsible for the lives of thirteen men. He was ordered one day to take and secure an area north of the U.S. Firebase in Da Nang, which was controlled by Viet Cong troops. Jim Weaver, his forward observer, crawled up a mud path to a hill overlooking the target zone fifty yards ahead when all hell broke loose. Hundreds of Cong troops came out from everywhere, surrounding Brian's men. As Brian called in for air support, Jim took a few shots, one through his shoulder and one in his stomach. F-105s arrived quickly and forced back the enemy. Right then Brian felt that hot sensation in his stomach, often described by others as the pain of a bullet twisting in his belly. Brian lifted Jim on his shoulders and carried him over to the med-evac helicopter which came in behind the assault jets. They both were rushed to a MASH unit in the area, all the time Brian comforting Jim in his arms. Before they reached the field hospital, Brian felt Jim's spirit leave his body and knew Jim did not make it. Brian was immediately taken into surgery to repair the damage he received in combat.

*****

My courthouse was situated in the City of Rochester, downtown across the park from the city hall and police department. Their small police department patrolled the downtown area, while the county sheriff's department patrolled the larger outer parts of Rochester Hills. When I began practicing law in the city, one large law firm seemed to represent everyone. As I said before, it was tough breaking into the law business in this little town. But now, I was one of the two judges presiding over a 200 square mile judicial district of which the city was a tiny part. The city attorney was the son of one of the original partners of that one large law firm. He was the type of person who was really all about himself, like many second-generation sons who do little to obtain their station in life. One of the city cops was a guy by the name of Bill Duke. Bill was a local boy, raised and educated in the city. After high school, he went directly to work for the police department. An urban legend persists that Officer Bill pulled his girlfriend's car over one day using his lights and siren. She told him she wanted to break off their relationship. Bill dragged her out of the car and threw her across the trunk of his patrol vehicle to give her a lecture, right out there in public for everyone to see. Bill had a personality that was very tightly wound, not one who should be allowed to carry a gun.

By this time, many years had gone by since graduating from law school. With all the attorneys practicing in the tri-county area, I rarely saw a classmate practicing in my out-county courtroom. One morning, however, a familiar face of a fellow student checked into the clerk's office for a case scheduled on my docket. He was directed to a conference room where the city attorney was preparing cases before going into the courtroom. This was the first time in a long time a friend from law school had an opportunity to appear before me. He entered the conference room where several attorneys and police officers sat around a large table. The city attorney asked him his client's name. He responded, "Brian Nelson." Quickly as in a knee jerk reaction, the city attorney reacted "Oh, that asshole." Bill Duke sitting across the table let out a strident laugh. Brian's lawyer was shocked and without words. Where was the decorum? Where was the civil respect? Where were the moral principles? His blood started to boil, but he maintained his outward cool.

Brian Nelson drove through Rochester's downtown one night about 9:30 where his car was stopped by Officer Bill Duke. Brian provided his license and proof of insurance as requested by the officer, who returned to his patrol vehicle to run the driver's record on the computer. Brian was on his way home and needed to relieve himself often because of his missing spleen and damaged bladder, a keepsake of the Vietnam War. He stepped out of his car and walked behind a closed and darkened used car lot and took a leak. Officer Duke became enraged with Brian, as if he were a fleeing felon. The angered officer put the driver through all of those nasty sobriety tests, touching your nose and heal-to-toe walk in a straight line right out there in the public where everyone could see. Brian's heal-to-toe walk test took place on a downhill sidewalk. He did not do well with this test because of the leg braces he wore every day since receiving them in the military hospital. Brian was arrested and charged with Drunken Driving and Indecent Exposure.

A hearing date was set for a motion to dismiss the indecent exposure case, because Brian's lawyer believed the city's ordinance was unconstitutional. He argued that the ordinance in question was so vague no one was able to understand the law and the court must dismiss the case. The arrogant city attorney looked down his glasses at defense counsel as he rose to address the court. "Your Honor," he began, "What if my mother was looking out the window when this person was urinating down there between the cars? Better yet, what if my little sister was looking out the window when all this took place?" I knew as a matter of fact that it was pitch-black dark outside and no lights illuminated the closed used car lot. No one was able to see anything! I thought I would bring a little insight to the moment. "Mr. City Attorney, what if you were looking out the window? Would you see this act to be indecent?" Any exposure was solely in the mind of the city attorney.

It is never a good idea to get involved with the local government's internal business by declaring one of their ordinances unconstitutional, unless you really have to do it. The city attorney was unresponsive to my question. His silence said a lot about his legal position. I gave these arguments full consideration. I presumed if one charge could be resolved and knocked out by this ruling, the lawyers would certainly be able to settle the drunken driving part of the case. But no, I did not appreciate the degree of animosity that had developed between these two legal warriors. Finally, I hedged my decision and ruled that the writers of the ordinance never contemplated this unique situation; thus the ordinance was inapplicable in only this case. The Indecency charge was no longer part of the case. The city attorney stormed out of the court with disapproval and a date was set for selecting the jury to hear the drunken driving case.

Months later Brian Nelson and his same trial lawyer appeared again in court ready to select a jury and try the drunken driving case. Seeing Brian reminded the city attorney of their earlier encounter, causing the hairs on the back of his head to bristle. This trial would test of the strengths of each of these seasoned trial attorneys. The city attorney was raised in this small town. He was a local boy like Duke and now owned the respect of all the public officials and, in his mind, most of the residents. Brian's lawyer took this case on like all his previous case as a challenge—a fight to the finish. Ever since his childhood days scrimmaging in the streets, he was the type of person whose mouth immediately exposed every thought his brain ever had. The jury was selected, I was ready and the court was finally called to order. The bailiff announced, "People of the City of Rochester versus Brian Nelson. Mr. City Attorney, call your first witness."

Bill Duke was the first and only one to take the witness stand. He described the night of the arrest as best he could remember. The speed limit on Main Street going up the hill was 25 mph. He stated how Nelson disappeared behind the used cars after presenting his license. Duke described conducting alcohol sobriety tests with Nelson on the sidewalk next to his patrol car. Brian was unable to walk a straight line in the heal-to-

toe test, so Duke arrested him for operating a motor vehicle while being intoxicated. That essentially completed the City's case. Brian's lawyer did not think the City presented enough evidence to support a conviction; so he asked me to dismiss the case at that point. I felt otherwise. In jury trials, it is the responsibility of the jury to decide what the facts of the case are and how they apply to the law. It is the judge's job to tell the jury which laws they should apply to the facts, as they find them to be.

The fundamental nature of a jury trial is being honest with the jury. During jury selection, we come across many of our neighbors who are very good people. As they are selected out of the large group (the array) and placed into a new unit (the jury panel), they become strong and willing to listen to the many troublesome and often conflicting facts in a trial. The jury becomes more dedicated to their responsibilities as the trial progresses. They are able to see through the language of the lawyers and set aside the hubris connected to the actors. In short, they want to make the right decisions for all the right reasons.

Brian Nelson took the witness stand to tell his side of the story. Brian said he was not speeding and there was no real reason for the officer to stop and arrest him. He admitted he was having trouble walking that evening. Softly and gently his lawyer opened the door to the past. In answer to the next question, Brian told the story of being drafted into the Army just after graduating from high school in the late sixties. He described how he was quickly promoted to platoon leader and shipped off to Vietnam after basic training, alongside thousands of other young men his age. Brian described the various battles he was involved in with his men, supposedly defending our country here from over there. He then described the day he was on patrol when the North Vietnamese overran his platoon's position. He recounted that day on the way to the hospital after being shot and how his buddy Jim Weaver died in his arms. His lawyer then asked Brian to stand up in the witness stand. Brian explained the reasons he could not walk very well that evening and complete the test for the officer. He then showed the jury the braces he brought home as another remembrance of the war. His well-spoken lawyer said nothing more as he turned slowly towards the jurors, looked each one of them directly in the eye without saying what was on his mind. And in a soft tone as he rotated towards the bench, he softly said, "Your Honor, I rest my case." The silence in the courtroom was palpable.

The jury deliberated for just over twenty minutes before returning a favorable verdict of "not guilty". The jury humbled the arrogant city attorney, but he never lost any of his self-importance. Bill Duke grumbled a little while leaving the courtroom. He got back into his police car and continued his career harassing kids and intimidating others in the name of protecting the community. The victorious lawyer consumed with the jury verdict said with a grin to Brian, "I'm just sayin', how good was that?" He soon left the courthouse without coming back to my chambers and speaking to me. I never saw him after that; but he sure did a good job for Brian Nelson while he was in the courtroom.

**And then there is this...**
And the end draws near. It is easy to tell the end when the pages of a novel begin to run short and you only hope the book has a great ending.

Winter comes to an end in the South during the months of February and March when the azaleas burst into gorgeous blooms; finally exhausting themselves as their petals fall onto the warm spring soil. Summer ends with the brilliant fall colors which once again return us to winter.

The Michigan Supreme Court approved a State Bar petition to create a new Emeritus membership status for senior lawyers effective October 1, 2004.

The Supreme Court order states that an active or inactive State Bar member who is 70 years or older or who has been a member for at least 30 years, may elect Emeritus status so long as there are no pending disciplinary actions against the member in any state. Emeritus status members are exempt from paying Bar

Association dues. They can no longer practice law in Michigan, but are eligible to receive other member benefits.

Now, after forty-five years as a member of the Michigan Bar Association, I will take the soft landing and elect Emeritus status at the end of this year. So as the conclusion draws near, I wish you my best wishes going forward, memories of the ups and downs and the experiences of my life and career in the Law.

Hon. James P. Sheehy
District Judge Emeritus.

# Conclusion

"It is my pleasure and honor as Mayor of the City of Rochester Hills to hereby commend and recognize the Honorable James P. Sheehy, District Court Judge, for his long distinguished public service to the community and his valuable contributions to Michigan's jurisprudence and the County and State bench and bar.

"Judge Sheehy's tenure on the court has been distinguished by his professional demeanor and his thoughtful truth-seeking approach to each case that came before him. Judge Sheehy was blessed, and in turn, blessed the community, with his ability to extract a fair and just interpretation or conclusion from the voluminous and often cumbersome compilations of laws, codes and regulations he had to apply. Perhaps most remarkable and distinctive about Judge Sheehy is his nature to always weigh and take into account the individual circumstances of the persons who appeared before him in order to avert the unduly harsh consequences that may sometimes result from a strict, literal or mechanical application of the rule or regulation.

"Judge Sheehy brought to the judiciary a uniquely compassionate and humane approach that enabled him to reconcile the law and the public purpose it is designed to facilitate with the realities and hardships of life. The trait was most evident when little David was confronted by mighty Goliath in Judge Sheehy's court. Judge Sheehy always made sure that David received a fair day in court.

"The residents of Rochester Hills will surely miss; but will also fondly remember and appreciate Judge Sheehy's innate sense of fairness and honesty and his long standing commitment to public service, and on behalf of the City of Rochester Hills, I wish him peace, good health and prosperity in his retirement and future endeavors."

Mayor Somerville, City of Rochester Hills, Michigan, 2000

---

The small oceanfront town on the southeast coast, the same town where the dreadful poker player's trial took place, became a regular vacation spot. My judicial schedule allowed me to take a break from work and the weather up North two or three times a year. After attending a one-week seminar on the subject of Mediation offered by the National Judicial College in a city nearby, my life began to change. Each day for a week, I got up to have a coffee and roll and drive downtown to my classes. How bad could it be living here full time, I wondered.

I began to appreciate the slower pace of life in the South, along with the warmer weather. During a family vacation in 1999, I looked around for a small place to hang my hat and leave some clothes between visits. A friend showed me a small bungalow spec home that had just been completed. I drove over and walked through the newly finished residence. This house reminded me of my current home. In fact, the town was reminiscent of Rochester where we first moved thirty years earlier. I made an offer on the home which was accepted. For the first time in my life, I was the owner of two homes located in different states.

Having an adequate number of years of service on the bench, my age allowed me to retire with full benefits. One more trip to visit the new home in the oceanfront town for some final calculations and that was it! I decided to retire and put my escape plan into action.

There is a procedure for announcing a judicial retirement. The retirement declaration must be made in a window of time, no greater than ninety days, or less than thirty days, before the actual date of retirement. The Monday after the Thanksgiving weekend, I publicly announced I would be stepping down from the bench the first week in January. I do not have to tell you what a big surprise this notice was to everyone in the courthouse and the community.

I wanted to clear out as many pending cases as possible before leaving the bench, so I reset most of the awaiting files for new pretrial conferences. This was a good way to get many of the attorneys from the county to make one more swing through my chambers in order to say goodbye. My wife called this process, "a walk down memory lane." I was very amenable to just about any plea bargain that came along. I even sweetened some deals to get the cases closed. This was known by the practicing attorneys as "wholesale day at the flea market." I accomplished my goal and reduced the court backlog to nothing. That is the way I wanted to leave the court.

Plans for a retirement party started to appear. I had something in mind; similar to everyone going over to the Hamlin Pub one day after work and hoisting a cold one. I just wanted to avoid the expense and all the fanfare I envisioned in the meaning of a retirement party. A happy medium was agreed upon. Plans shifted from the Legion Hall to the log cabin house in the city park. The administrator made arrangements with a caterer to prepare a nice food table and the Pub to provide the liquid refreshments. It ultimately looked like a Super Bowl party, where all the drinks were on the house.

My wife and I greeted all the guests who arrived at the front door. The large number of people, in excess of 200, that showed up overwhelmed me. The presiding judge began some official remarks while plaques and proclamations began flowing like the tap beer at the portable bar in the main room. The state senator presented me with a joint resolution of the legislature signed by the governor. A similar resolution was presented by the state representative and another from the Chief Judge of the Court. Just when I thought the presentations were over and I could get back to the party, the mayor asked to say a few words.

Mayor Somerville handed me the keys to the city, declared this day as *Judge James P. Sheehy Day* in the City of Rochester Hills and then she recited her proclamation. I could not have said it any better, even if I wrote the proclamation myself.

### And finally, there is this...

As I said in the opening, my first thought in writing this book was to share these stories with those that may be interested in a career in the Law. Sometimes the journey is longer than you would think. One should always remember though...Never give up on your dreams. Where ever your dreams take you, go with them. Frank Sinatra said it best in his rendition of his famous song...*That's Life*.

*I've been a puppet, a pauper, a pirate,*
*A poet, a pawn and a king.*
*I've been up and down and over and out*
*But I know one thing:*
*Each time I find myself flat on my face,*
*I pick myself up and get back in the race.*

*That's Life Lyrics,* Writer: Dean Kay, Kelly L. Gordon

# Endnotes

Chapter One
<u>In Defense of the Corpus Delicti Rule</u>, Moran, 64 Ohio State Journal 817
Courtroom Handbook on Michigan Evidence, 2008, ICLE, Ann Arbor, MI.

Chapter Two

Chapter Three

Chapter Four
Michigan Rules of Professional Conduct, 6.5, Conduct, 1988, ammended10-01-1993

Chapter Five
*People v Sites*, Mich Court of Appeals, #57736, Nov. 22, 1982
*The Myth of Prosecutorial Accountability*, The Yale Law Journal Online, yalelawjournal.org, Nov 2011.
New York Times, OPINION by Raymond Bonner March 4, 2012, page 8
Wall Street Journal, Opinion, *Department of Injustice*, March 17, 2012. Page A14
Anatomy of Injustice, *A Murder Case Gone Wrong*, Raymond Bonner, 2012 Alfred A. Kropf

Chapter Six
See: Star of Past Charged of Stealing Small Town's Hope for the Future, New York Times, published December 31, 1996, www.nytimes .com

Chapter Seven
"Dancing in the Moonlight" is the title song on the 1973 King Harvest album *Dancing in the Moonlight*, written by Sherman Kelly, 1968
<u>Effect of Violence of Laws and Policies Facilitating the Transfer of Juveniles from the Juvenile Justice System to the Adult Justice System</u>, Am J Prev Med, 2007; 32(4s;s7s28)

Chapter Eight
*Tumey v State of Ohio* (1927) 273 US 510 at 523
*Caperton v A. T. Massey Coal Co.* (2009) 556 US \_\_\_\_, Docket #08-22

State Court Passes 1st Test of Bias Rules, Editorial, *Detroit Free Press*, 2-03-10, Pg. A-8
Also read, *The Appeal*, by John Grisham

Chapter Nine

Chapter Ten
Fredrick Lauck is a friend from the old neighborhood. He related this story of Judge Kelley to me and with permission shared his notes from his introduction speech given at her Swearing-In Ceremony.
How the World Sees Detroit, Opinion, *Detroit Free Press*, Nolan Finley, 10-22-2009
Yogi Berra: *The Clinician-Educator's Notebook*
www.bcm.edu/pediatrics/?pmid-1620

Chapter Eleven
Fredrick Lauck tried a criminal case of the *People v Michael Wade* in the Wayne County Circuit Court. From the transcript and trial notes, this story is told with his permission.
After the Fall, Cameron McWhirter, WSJ, November 9, 2012
*Wall Street Journal*, Opinion, Motown's Mental Breakdown, December 4, 2012

Chapter Twelve
*The Docket*, University of Detroit School of Law, Fall, 2006, Pages 4-9

Chapter Thirteen
Eye in the Sky lyrics © Universal Music Publishing Group

Chapter Fourteen

Chapter Fifteen
Michigan Historical Archives

Chapter Sixteen
The Barbie Bandits Get Busted, Newsweek, published March 12, 2000, Philip Mathew
*Who's Looking Out for You?* Bill O'Reilly, 2003, Random House, Inc.

Chapter Seventeen
Las Vegas Review-Journal, The Editorials, Asset seizure, August 26, 2011
*Bennis v Michigan* (1996) 516 US 442, March 4, 1996
Grandholm Commutes Clarkston Man's Drug Sentences, *Detroit Free Press*, L.L. Brasier, 10-11-2008

Chapter Eighteen
Fred Lauck contributed colorful background to this chapter along with comments on the Insanity Defense.
*The Caveman* by Aram "Rocky" Alkazoff, CBZ Journal, Nov. 2000, www.cyberboxing zone.com/boxing/wail1100_rocky
Rocky Balboa, 2006, movie written by Sylvester Stallone
*Gideon v. Wainwright*, 372 US 335 (1963)
Caveman Lee reminds all of Emanuel Steward's good deeds, Shawn Windsor, Detroit Free Press, November 14, 2012

See Rocky's State Prison Mug Shot
http://mdocweb.state.mi.us/OTIS2/otis2profile.aspx?mdoc Number=186977

Chapter Nineteen
http://www.stargazette.com/VideoNetwork/1966700450001/Woman-holds-only-an-idiot-sign-for-driving-around-bus?odyssey=mod|video||life

Chapter Twenty
Facilitation, *Latches,* Oakland County Bar Association, 2000

Chapter Twenty One
*Examining Issues through Political Cartoons, The Vietnam War,* p 25.
*The Vietnam War* (Examining Issues through Political Cartoons) By Louise I. Gerdes

Conclusion
"That's Life Lyrics" Writer: Dean Kay, Kelly L. Gordon

(c) Copyright---J. Sheehy, 2014

*Except as provided under the Copyright Act, no part of this publication may be reproduced, stored in a retrieval system or transmitted in any form or by any means without the prior permission of the author and publisher.*

# Acknowledgments

*"This is the City*
*Los Angeles, California.*
*Some people rob for pleasure,*
*Some rob just because it is there.*
*You never know.*

*"My name is Friday; I'm a Cop.*
*I was working the day watch out of Robbery*
*When I got the call..."* Jack Webb, *Dragnet*

---

Thank you Mother for my Jesuit education during the age of the Dragnet TV programs and my formative educational years at the University of Detroit Jesuit High School.

Luck, they say, is found at the intersection of preparation and opportunity. Being able to work for Chief Justice Tom Brennan who introduced me to former Justice and now Federal Circuit Judge Jim Ryan is the luck I'm talking about. They have remained my friends throughout my career.

I gratefully acknowledge Fred Lauck, a classmate from grade school, college and law school, who shared his trial practices and reminiscences while challenging me to write this book.

Thanks to my wife Katy for proofreading and correcting my grammar where it needed correcting. Thanks also to my daughter Doctor and Professor Colleen for assisting me with the English language and computer settings.

Thanks to our friends at Accu Print Inc. for the first proofs that headed me down the pathway of correct style and form.

My nineteen years on the bench were greatly enhanced by my court officer, Tom Cattel, my secretary-court recorder Diane Apel and all my clerks, including Mendy Balian. They too have remained loyal friends.

www.ingramcontent.com/pod-product-compliance
Lightning Source LLC
Chambersburg PA
CBHW020855180526
45163CB00007B/2511